Yves Saint Laurent & Art

General editors: Madison Cox, Stephan Janson and Mouna Mekouar

All works by Yves Saint Laurent featured in this book are
from the collections of the Musée Yves Saint Laurent Paris.

Captions are listed in chronological order of works presented
within museum permanent collections.

All exhibition photographs are by Nicolas Mathéus.

Yves Saint Laurent & Art

Centre Pompidou
Musée d'Art Moderne de Paris
Musée du Louvre
Musée d'Orsay
Musée National Picasso, Paris
Musée Yves Saint Laurent Paris

from Y. S. L.
Amicalement A. M. C.
62

Foreword

On the eve of the 60th anniversary of the first collection by the House of Yves Saint Laurent, which was shown on 4 December 1961, it is with immense pride and gratitude that we inaugurate a series of innovative installations at six of the most prestigious fine arts museums in Paris. They will pay homage to the extraordinary creative talent of the late French couturier, Yves Saint Laurent.

Sixty years ago, the twenty-six-year-old Yves Saint Laurent and thirty-two-year-old Pierre Bergé launched a venture that would establish Saint Laurent as one of the most inventive and influential fashion designers of the second half of the 20th century.

The unique dialogue that existed between Yves Saint Laurent and the myriad sources of inspiration he found in the fine arts, spanning a vast range of cultures throughout history, was a key component of the couturier's ingenuity and boundless creativity.

What more fitting manner to celebrate this 60th anniversary than to bring together these six renowned French cultural institutions – a ground-breaking event in and of itself – and offer an incisive look at the work of one of France's greatest fashion innovators alongside pieces from these esteemed museums' permanent collections.

On behalf of the Fondation Pierre Bergé–Yves Saint Laurent, the curators Mouna Mekouar and Stephan Janson, and the entire team at the Musée Yves Saint Laurent Paris, I remain deeply grateful to all the participating museum institutions and their staff for embracing this ingenious and avant-garde approach to looking at fashion and artistic expression.

Madison Cox
President
Fondation Pierre Bergé-Yves Saint Laurent

[Opposite] Cassandre (Adolphe Jean-Marie Mouron),
logo for the Yves Saint Laurent couture house, 1961.

Contents

'My weapon is the way
I look at my times
and the art of my times.'[1]
Yves Saint Laurent

Introduction:
Yves Saint Laurent and Art

Mouna Mekouar

[p. 8] Yves Saint Laurent in his apartment in the place Vauban, Paris, 1960s.

In 1962 – sixty years ago – Yves Saint Laurent designed his first collection under his own name. It was a bolt from the blue. A sign that things were about to change. 'That morning is one I shall never forget [...]. I realized that something had happened,'[2] Pierre Bergé said years later, referring to the collection show on 29 January 1962. The press went into raptures: 'Yves Saint Laurent has succeeded in giving the idiosyncrasies of his time a wholly aristocratic look.'[3] That first collection was a determining moment in Yves Saint Laurent's career. He had set himself apart, not only from the man who had taught him, Christian Dior, but also from Schiaparelli, Chanel and Balenciaga. He was free at last, free to be himself. Couture became a form of conquest, a challenge – to invent fashions that reflected a new way of looking at the world. 'I wanted to create a fashion that was absolutely pure,' he said. 'I designed a very simple collection [...]. The clothes were very close-fitting and simply enhanced the body's natural shape. That was it: there were no decorative additions, nothing else. Line was everything,' he explained when a new collection was released in 1975. 'I suddenly realized that what I was looking for, in essence, needed to be like a Brancusi. I wanted something like those rising layers of metal, those "birds". Women should have that kind of silhouette. A little like those Brancusi sculptures, anyway. In truth, there are multiple connections between art and me!'[4] He recognized that forms are universal and cannot be compartmentalized, and throughout his career – from 1962 to 2002 – he continued to make these connections with art, establishing both a spirit and a style.

Yves Saint Laurent was a highly cultured man and in his work he was able to look beyond his immediate world to other times and places. He was fond of literature and particularly fond of Proust, immersing himself repeatedly in the pages of *À la recherche du temps perdu*, which he was unable to bring himself to quite finish. Proust came to inhabit his life, his work and his writing, and unsurprisingly this passion for Proust found its way into his designs, in various guises. Like the writer himself, Yves Saint Laurent was living in a world in transition. 'I was torn between fascination for the past and the future that was driving me on. It feels as if I am split in two and I think I always will be. Because I know one world and sense the presence of the other,'[5] he said.

The Proustian influences that permeate his work – and his life – foreshadow, by extension, the fashion transformations reflected through the prism of gender and expressed in Yves Saint Laurent's masculine/feminine, day/evening dialectic, which resulted in the smoking jacket and suit being widely adopted as womenswear. 'As far as I am concerned, there is nothing more beautiful than a woman wearing men's clothes! Because all her femininity comes into play,'[6] he said. This idea of playing with fashion's rules prefigured, in condensed form, the approach that Yves Saint Laurent would adopt throughout his career, in countless variations.

Yves Saint Laurent was familiar not just with the work of Proust but also with the poetry of Apollinaire, Louis Aragon and Cocteau, and embroidered fragments of their verse appeared on coats he designed in 1980. He was equally passionate about cinema, music and theatre. There was one area of artistic endeavour, however, that eclipsed the rest and to which he kept returning: painting. Painting is Ariadne's thread, helping us to find our way through Yves Saint Laurent's labyrinth. 'I have always loved painting', he said, 'and so it was inevitable that it should inspire my creations.'[7] He was an avid collector who filled his home with works by Brancusi, Léger, De Chirico, Ingres, Klee, Cézanne, Picasso, Mondrian, Goya and many others. This contact with what we might describe as the 'Absolute' in his daily life was, for Yves Saint Laurent, perhaps a way of counterbalancing the transitory nature of fashion.

As well as a private art collection, Yves Saint Laurent also owned a library. Partially dispersed today, it contained thousands of books, a testament to the wealth and diversity of the couturier's sources of inspiration. 'I have just started working at home, sitting at a desk, which serves that purpose and no other,' he said. 'The room consists of a mirror, a sofa and two bookcases. Those bookcases contain all the reserves I could wish to draw on.'[8] Yves Saint Laurent regarded his library as an interactive space, a repository of images. Each book allowed him to intuit the world in a new way. 'I flick through them [...] and then feel a spontaneous creative urge. It's a wonderful moment.'[9] His library was a

This non-exhaustive selection demonstrates Yves Saint Laurent's many fields of artistic interest, and his ability to embrace varied cultures and civilizations as influences for his own creations.

1. *Ushabti* funerary box, showing a musician worshipping Osiris, c. 1295–1069 BCE, Egypt, painted wood and stucco, Musée du Louvre. 2. Yves Saint Laurent, gown worn by Shiraz Tal, Autumn–Winter 1998–99, photograph by Guy Marineau. 3. *Aphrodite and Eros*, Roman Empire, marble, Musée du Louvre. 4. Yves Saint Laurent, gown worn by Natalia Semanova, Spring–Summer 1999.

5. *Karomama, Divine Adoratrice of Amun*, 22th dynasty (c. 945–715 BCE), Egypt, bronze, Musée du Louvre, Paris.   6. Yves Saint Laurent, evening gown worn by Luciana, Spring–Summer 1967, photograph by Jacques Verroust.   7. The Menelaus Painter, wine krater, c. 450–440 BCE, ceramic, Musée du Louvre, Paris.   8. Yves Saint Laurent, Grecian-style evening gown worn by Elsa Faúndez de Dodero, Spring–Summer 1971, photograph by Jean Michel.

9. François Boucher, *Madame de Pompadour*, c. 1750, oil on paper, Musée du Louvre, Paris.   10. Yves Saint Laurent, evening gown worn by Magali Lemoine, Spring–Summer 1994, photograph by Guy Marineau.   11. Frans Hals the Elder, *Paulus van Beresteyn*, 1581/85–1666, oil on canvas, Musée du Louvre.   12. Yves Saint Laurent, evening gown worn by Sabrina Magalhaes, Autumn–Winter 2000–1.

13. Sandro Botticelli, *The Virgin and Child (Madonna of the Guidi da Faenza)*, 1444/45–1510, oil on wood, Musée du Louvre, Paris.   14. Yves Saint Laurent, 'Botticelli' bridal gown, worn by Sylvie Gueguen, Autumn–Winter 1989–90.   15. Antoine Watteau, *The Two Cousins*, c. 1716–17, oil on canvas, Musée du Louvre, Paris.   16. Yves Saint Laurent, 'Watteau' gown, worn by Cindy McDermott, Spring–Summer 1990.

'virtual museum' which he constantly explored as a prompt to his own creative processes. 'If I read a book, with photographs, about India, or about Egypt – somewhere I have never been – I am transported in my imagination. That's where my finest journeys take place.'[10] His art books opened up the whole world for him. Yves Saint Laurent's library vividly demonstrates how his vision of artistic creation was enriched by civilizations from around the world. Of his virtual museum, he said: 'A museum is a living place. Creativity – the creativity of artists now dead or unknown – is always a living thing, too.'[11]

'I admire ancient art for its novelty,'[12] Tristan Tzara once said. The couturier appears to have felt something very similar about time and great works of art: 'I wanted to transform all of that. Because I was torn between fascination for the past and the future that was driving me on.'[13] It was a question not merely of influence but of a different paradigm, new fields of awareness. For Yves Saint Laurent, cultural references were a way of returning to his own times and expressing himself in the present tense. 'I didn't copy them – who would venture to do that?' he said. 'I wanted to weave connections between the painting and the clothing, since I believe that a painter is always of our time and can be part of the life of each and every one of us.'[14] He did *not* copy. He constantly reinterpreted and reworked. It was a process of constant renewal, from one season to the next – referencing Mondrian in 1965, Wesselmann and Pop art in 1966, Picasso in 1979, Matisse in 1980, Braque in 1988, and so on. Yves Saint Laurent was always mirroring art, subtly, in his fashions. 'It was in 1968; the year I exposed an actual breast, like the *Victory of Samothrace*,'[15] said the man who was inspired as much by ancient Greek and Egypt and the civilizations of India, China and Africa as he was by Van Gogh, Watteau, Ingres, Delacroix and Vermeer. 'You will always find an *infanta* or a *maja* somewhere in my collections,'[16] he said, referencing Velázquez and Goya.

The truth is that Yves Saint Laurent dramatically changed the relationship between art and fashion. His 'Homage to Mondrian' dresses (p. 55) were something of a manifesto. They conveyed the power of the original works while transforming them into three-dimensional objects. 'I suddenly realized that we needed to stop thinking of a piece of clothing as a sculpture and view it instead as a moving structure,'[17] he said. He had the ability to switch from plane to volume, surface aesthetic to body aesthetic. Pictorial representation was integral: it gave structure to the garment; it was an act of construction, not illustration. This transformation changed the object and its status: 'It is not because of the fashion that has been derived from it and relayed across the globe but because these dresses have helped to introduce the general public to a major forgotten artist, one who, to my way of thinking, took the concept of purity furthest in the 20th century.'[18] These dresses and others like them are part of a plan, rather than an idea. What we are seeing is not a concept, a mental representation applied to fashion, but instead a way of looking at the world.

This 'way of looking' involves both anticipation and memory, perception and interpretation of the world. It is worth noting that Yves Saint Laurent's 1979 collection was designed three months before the landmark exhibition celebrating the donation of many Picasso works to the French State (which led to the founding of the Musée Picasso). 'At the Bibliothèque Nationale, I saw an exhibition of the scale models of Diaghilev's sets for his ballets.,' he recalled. 'My collection is based on that specific moment and constructed like a ballet. I used Picasso and a softer form of Cubism, the Harlequins, the Blue Period, the Rose Period, the *Tricorne* period, as my starting point.'[19] In 1988, Yves Saint Laurent set himself a challenge – to adapt the language of Cubism to couture, borrowing the concepts of dismantling and deconstruction from Braque and Picasso and transposing them into a field of endeavour synonymous, by definition, with rigorous construction and the harmonious interplay of flat surfaces. It was a paradox he resolved by attempting to 'set static things in motion on the body of a woman'.[20] Working at the interface of these two worlds – Cubism and couture – the following year, 1989, Yves Saint Laurent created a strikingly original collection full of energy and drama, demonstrating his brilliant ability to blend genres and techniques.

This collection, combining passion and excess, showed a different side to Yves Saint Laurent: his love of glamour and glitter. He loved embroidery and would often turn simple cardigan jackets into visions of pure light. His first gold-embroidered cardigan – the 'colour of the sun', as the couturier himself described it – shone like a halo in 1972, heralding the many future creations that were designed to be ornaments as well as garments. The use of a mixture of rich and humble materials to create such glitzy formalwear was a bold move indeed. By borrowing from the past – both forms and systems of belief – these designs also came to be endowed with particular cultural, symbolic and historical meaning.

Yves Saint Laurent reclaimed, reinterpreted and realigned; he was provocative and he broke the rules. It was by following these principles that he created his collections. From one metamorphosis to the next, chronology meant nothing; he was governed only by the logic of his imagination. In one and the same collection, he would weave striking correspondences, orchestrated using a system of references that were lost amid the processes of creation. 'Oh! There are so many!' the couturier declared. 'In Vélazquez's paintings, for example, the dresses are like oceans. In Manet's, I admire the sumptuous, nuanced whites, like those of the dress[es] in *The Balcony*. I find Pre-Raphaelite women sublime, very modern, and already liberated.'[21] Yves Saint Laurent was capable of evoking the golden age of Dutch painting or picking out details which, once transposed to the realm of couture, could just as easily be a reference to Picasso as Delaunay. And, just as Giacometti was bowled over by the discovery of African art, Yves Saint Laurent offered a totemic and hallucinatory vision of the female body for his Spring–Summer 1967 collection (p. 49). Each of his creations is the location for a secret conversation, a kind of silent meeting place where different perspectives and time periods intersect. The same is true for his colour palette, which reflects his own interpretations of the palette of Bonnard and Matisse, as well as his concepts of 'Veronese green', 'Frans Hals black', and more. For Yves Saint Laurent, colour is expression. It is not something that completes a design; it is a theme and a medium in itself.

The couturier, like Andy Warhol, whom he admired, took a free and playful attitude to the boundaries between fine art and applied art, between art and fashion, and between the unique and the mass-produced. During his own lifetime, rules were already being broken in relation to art and life with the emergence of performance art, happenings and new media. Yves Saint Laurent carefully stage-managed his own work, creating through his fashion shows a dramatic narrative that was a work of art in itself.

Yves Saint Laurent left a massive archive comprising thousands of Polaroids recording the making of his fashion shows. These images – shot by various people, often studio assistants – enabled the couturier to capture the look he was after. They were tools of the trade, but today they could well be regarded – like Warhol's Polaroids – as works of art in their own right. Capturing fleeting moments while work was still progress, they are precious evidence of the creative fever engendered by each collection. 'You need time, and a great deal of humility, to succeed. Everyone who works hard is appreciated here. We are fortunate in that respect. He looks. We all understand his silences, his emotions. It is his natural courtesy speaking when he says "your skirt is sublime, Madame Jacqueline" or "what a beautifully sewn sleeve",'[22] explained Anne-Marie Muñoz, his studio manager. Yves Saint Laurent produced huge quantities of sketches when he was designing his collections. These sketches were the creative impetus for the entire atelier, which transposed and crafted at every stage of the process, turning the designs into reality. The whole fashion house was involved in the metamorphoses orchestrated by the couturier. 'This is my firm and it's a great joy to feel so much love from it,' he said. 'I am talking of the female staff, the *premières*, the whole house. It's a house that's based on love.'[23] In 1990, Yves Saint Laurent designed a jacket entitled 'Homage to My House' (p. 165). It embodied the love he felt for his couture house, but also his belief that artistic creation is an infinite thing that never stays still. Embroidered all over with rock crystal to symbolize purity, the jacket was a glittering ornament that changed from moment to moment depending on the effects of the light. 'What I love most is behaving as if I could sculpt light,' the couturier said. 'It's as if I were a painter, or a writer.'[24] Ultimately, every one of his collections was a portrait of the artist – a self-portrait.

17. Francisco Goya, *Portrait of Mariana Waldstein, Ninth Marquesa of Santa Cruz*, 1797, oil on canvas, Musée du Louvre, Paris.   18. Yves Saint Laurent, evening gown worn by Kirat Young, Spring–Summer 1977.   19. Édouard Manet, *A Matador*, c. 1866–67, oil on canvas, Metropolitan Museum of Art, New York.   20. Yves Saint Laurent, 'Torero' evening ensemble, worn by Mounia Orosemane, Autumn–Winter 1979–80.

21. James Tissot, *The Ball*, 1878, oil on canvas, Musée d'Orsay, Paris.   22. Yves Saint Laurent, evening gown worn by Dothi Dumonteil, Autumn–Winter 1981–82.   23. Auguste Renoir, *The Swing*, 1876, oil on canvas, Musée d'Orsay, Paris.   24. Yves Saint Laurent, bridal gown worn by Natalia Semanova, Autumn–Winter 2000, photograph by Frédéric Bukajlo.

25. Henri Matisse, *Woman in Blue*, 1937, oil on canvas, Philadelphia Museum of Art.
26. Yves Saint Laurent, evening gown inspired by Henri Matisse, worn by Kirat Young,
Autumn–Winter 1981–82.   27. Georges Braque, *The Birds*, detail of the ceiling panels
in the former antechamber of Henri II, Musée du Louvre, Paris.   28. Yves Saint Laurent,
evening ensemble worn by Martian Royaards, Spring–Summer 1988.

Yves Saint Laurent's entire fashion career can be seen as a dialogue between his life, craft and experiences, and the life, craft and experiences of other artists. Exhibitions that celebrated his work were landmark moments in that career. Diana Vreeland, the so-called 'Empress of Fashion', launched the trend by lionizing the couturier, during his lifetime, at the Metropolitan Museum of Art in 1983. Other retrospectives were to follow – Beijing in 1985, Leningrad and Paris in 1986, and more. Today, sixty years after his first collection, how best can we celebrate the work of a couturier who had such a profound impact not only on his own century but on the following one too?

The exhibition 'Yves Saint Laurent aux musées' establishes a different kind of dialogue – between the couturier's creations and individual artworks held in the collections at the Musée du Louvre, the Centre Pompidou, the Musée d'Orsay, the Musée Picasso and the Musée d'Art Moderne de Paris. These connections and cross-references enable us to revisit what may be seen as defining moments in a unique creative journey, and at the same time to celebrate great works of art from around the world. The works that have been selected represent moments in his career when Yves Saint Laurent asked questions, responded to new ideas, upset the status quo or expanded the horizons of fashion. The selection does not claim to be exhaustive. Other names, other works, could have been included, and the field of research could have been expanded, without affecting the fundamental theme of the exhibition – the inventiveness of an approach that is open to so many influences.

Based on this transhistorical and transcultural dynamic, the exhibition can be viewed as a chain of linked islands. It pays homage to the expertise and the people involved in the making of the Yves Saint Laurent brand. The goal of these different narratives is to create in each museum – including the Musée Yves Saint Laurent Paris – an opportunity to reflect on the couturier's work, to generate spheres of resonance and metaphor, to explore his ideas about art and his mythology. This mythology relates not only to the unfathomable part of him, the part he himself was unable to reach, but also his quest – his dream – to wed the absolute with the fleetingness of fashion.

Yves Saint Laurent's designs redefined the century in which they were created and continue to challenge our own. The couturier was constantly coming up with original ways of reinventing and reworking his sources of inspiration, and his innovative new designs in turn influenced the creative endeavours of his time. He helped to take art and fashion into a new era. 'Art like fashion reflects its time', he said, 'and it is quite normal for contemporary painting to influence fashion; unless it happens the other way around.'[25]

1. Yves Saint Laurent quoted in 'Yves Saint Laurent et l'art', *Air France Madame*, August 1990.
2. Pierre Bergé quoted in Laurence Benaïm, 'Introduction', in *Mode 1958–1990*, exh. cat., Karuizawa: Sezon Museum of Modern Art, 14 November–26 December 1990, p. 193.
3. Lucien François, *Combat*, 23 February 1962.
4. Yves Saint Laurent quoted in Christian Geelhaar, 'Mode-Kunst-Mode', *Tages-Anzeiger Magazin*, 20 December 1975 (interview conducted in French and published in German).
5. *Yves Saint Laurent par Yves Saint Laurent*, exh. cat., Paris: Musée des Arts de la Mode, 30 May–26 October 1986, Paris: Herscher/Musée des Arts de la Mode, p. 23.
6. Yves Saint Laurent, *Citations*, Paris: Les Éditions du Huitième Jour, 2010, p. 24.
7. Yves Saint Laurent, 'Mon dialogue avec l'art', in *Yves Saint Laurent. Dialogue avec l'art*, exh. cat., Paris: Fondation Pierre Bergé –Yves Saint Laurent, 10 March–31 October 2004.
8. Yves Saint Laurent quoted in 'Saint Laurent: 30 ans de passion', *Elle,* January 1992.
9. Yves Saint Laurent, 'Préface', in Nancy Hall-Duncan, *Histoire de la photographie de mode*, Paris: Chêne, 1978.
10. Yves Saint Laurent quoted in 'Je suis un homme scandaleux, finalement –Yves Saint Laurent par Catherine Deneuve', *Globe*, January 1986.
11. Yves Saint Laurent, handwritten notes on the renovation of two rooms at the National Gallery, London, bearing the names of Yves Saint Laurent and Pierre Bergé, 18 March 1998, archives of the Musée Yves Saint Laurent Paris.
12. Tristan Tzara, 'Manifeste Dada 1918', in *Dada est tatou. Tout est Dada*, introduction by Henri Béhar, Paris: Flammarion, 1996, p. 207.
13. Yves Saint Laurent, 'Préface', 1978, *op. cit.*
14. Yves Saint Laurent, 'Mon dialogue avec l'art', 2004, *op. cit.*
15. Yves Saint Laurent quoted in *L'Actualité*, 15 July 1991.
16. Yves Saint Laurent quoted in 'Yves Saint Laurent et l'art', 1990, *op. cit.*
17. Yves Saint Laurent quoted in Patrick Thévenon, 'Le couturier qui a pensé aux femmes d'aujourd'hui', *Candide*, 15 August 1965.
18. Yves Saint Laurent quoted in 'Yves Saint Laurent et l'art', 1990, *op. cit.*
19. Yves Saint Laurent quoted in *Vogue Paris*, September 1979.
20. Yves Saint Laurent quoted in Patrick Thévenon, 'Le choc Yves Saint Laurent', *Paris Match*, 12 February 1988.
21. Yves Saint Laurent quoted in 'Saint Laurent: 30 ans de passion', 1992, *op. cit.*
22. Anne-Marie Muñoz, quoted in 'L'esprit classique', in *Mode 1958–1990*, 1990, *op. cit.*, p. 201.
23. Yves Saint Laurent quoted in Laurence Benaïm, 'Mon plus grand défaut, c'est moi-même', *Dutch*, winter 1997.
24. Yves Saint Laurent quoted in 'La passion selon Saint Laurent', *L'Insensé*, November 1991.
25. Yves Saint Laurent quoted in 'Yves Saint Laurent et l'art', 1990, *op. cit.*

'I love other artists, but the ones that I've chosen were closest to my work, that's why I've called upon them. Mondrian, of course, who was the first one I dared to tackle in 1965 and whose strictness was designed to appeal to me, but also Matisse, Braque, Picasso, Bonnard, Léger. And how could I have resisted Pop art, which was the expression of my youth? Or Jasper Johns, Lichtenstein, Rauschenberg and my dearest Andy Warhol?'
Yves Saint Laurent

Yves Saint Laurent and the Musée National d'Art Moderne: A shared history

Christian Briend and Marie Sarré

[p. 22] Jeanloup Sieff, *Yves Saint Laurent*, 1971,
gelatin silver print, Centre Pompidou.

In 1974, the Yves Saint Laurent couture house moved from the rue Spontini, where it had been located since its creation in 1961, to 5 avenue Marceau, near the Musée National d'Art Moderne, which was housed in the Palais de Tokyo. This new physical proximity served to underline the close connection that already existed between the couturier and the great Paris institution.

As early as 1965, Yves Saint Laurent had demonstrated his interest in modern art by showing, as part of his Autumn–Winter collection, a set of cocktail dresses directly inspired by the work of Piet Mondrian – whose work he had discovered through Michel Seuphor's monograph, *Piet Mondrian, Life and Work* (1956). The principles of Neo-Plasticism, in which 'only pure relationships between pure constructive elements can result in pure beauty',[1] seemed, at that moment in time, to echo his vision of haute couture: a garment constructed like a piece of architecture, stripped of all ornament, designed to serve the modern woman. The fact that Yves Saint Laurent should choose Mondrian was to prove astonishingly far-sighted. Indeed, with the exception of an exhibition at the Galerie René Drouin in 1945 and a second at the Galerie Denise René in 1957, the work of this Dutch artist who died in New York in 1944 was still little known in France. None of his works had yet been acquired by any of France's public collections, with the exception of a posthumous lithograph presented to the Musée National d'Art Moderne by Seuphor in 1964.[2]

1. 'Homage to Piet Mondrian' dresses in front of *Composition with Red, Yellow, Blue and Black* (1921) by Piet Mondrian, Kunstmuseum Den Haag, The Hague, 12 January 1966, photograph by Eric Koch.

2 & 3. Pop art-inspired evening gown and cocktail dresses, Autumn–Winter 1966–67 collection, featured in 'Paris Fall Styles Full of Surprises', *Life*, 2 September 1966.

Four years later, in 1969, while the Musée de l'Orangerie was preparing to hold the first museum retrospective dedicated to Mondrian, a journalist writing in the weekly *Carrefour* noted: 'Having unjustly ignored him for 50 years, France is honouring the boldest rejuvenator of art this century has seen. [...] His doctrine has found multiple applications in the fields of architecture, the decorative arts and even haute couture.'[3] The Musée National d'Art Moderne, however, did not acquire its first work by Mondrian, *Composition in Red, Blue and White II* (1937; p. 54), until 1975, almost ten years after Yves Saint Laurent's Mondrian collection, and a year after his move to the avenue Marceau.[4]

The couturier, who said that his Mondrian dresses had 'helped to introduce the general public to a major forgotten artist',[5] would anticipate the museum's acquisitions on other occasions too. In the mid-1960s, when Pop art was still an unknown phenomenon in museums and galleries, despite the recent opening of the Galerie Ileana Sonnabend in Paris, Yves Saint Laurent showed an Autumn–Winter 1966–67 collection whose saturated colours recalled American Pop art and the French Nouveaux Réalistes. While the cocktail dresses echo motifs from Jim Dine (*Heart*, 1965; p. 65) and Roy Lichtenstein (*Sunrise*, 1965; p. 81), two wool jersey dresses – one short, printed with the profile of a woman's face with scarlet lips, the other full-length, bearing a nude female silhouette (p. 77) – are direct references to the 'Great American Nudes' painted by the American artist Tom Wesselmann. For *Life* magazine (figs. 2 & 3), the dresses were photographed in front of an oversized book of matches by Raymond Hains, like the one displayed in the couturier's first ready-to-wear boutique, Saint Laurent Rive Gauche, which opened on Paris's rue de Tournon in September 1966.

In 1967, it was to Op art that Yves Saint Laurent turned his attention, shortly before this style of visual art began to receive institutional recognition. That same year, the art historian Jean-Jacques Lévêque noted: 'Vasarely is all these things at once... the street abandoned to the pleasure of rhythm, walls invaded by a riot of colours that sing and multiply, and the new look of women who dress "Op", buy "Op", live "Op", sometimes perhaps without knowing that they do.'[6] Between 1967 and 1969, the textile house Maison Abraham supplied Yves Saint Laurent with printed fabricss (pp. 69–71) that were broadly inspired by this movement, which had been part of everyday life in France for almost a decade but had barely found its way into French institutions: the first works by Yaacov Agam did not join the collections of the Musée National d'Art Moderne until 1968, and Victor Vasarely's not until 1977, thanks to a gift from the artist.

Centre Pompidou

4. Yves Saint Laurent's farewell show, held at the
Centre Pompidou on 22 January 2002.

The opening of the Centre Pompidou in 1977 gave a new boost to the Musée National d'Art Moderne, enabling the creation of vast exhibition spaces devoted to contemporary art in addition to the establishment of a more cogent historical collection. Modernism was becoming part of France's cultural heritage, accompanied, in the worlds of fashion and the visual arts, by the emergence of a postmodern tendency. Between 1979 and 1988, Yves Saint Laurent's collections were created under the dual influences of Henri Matisse and Pablo Picasso. The couturier saw an exhibition devoted to the Ballets Russes at the Bibliothèque Nationale, and it was following this that a 'slightly soft Cubism',[7] of the kind seen in the ballets *Parade* and *Le Tricorne*, influenced his Autumn–Winter 1979–80 collection. An evening dress in satin crepe (p. 43) garnered attention through its similarity (in terms of both form and colour) to Picasso's *Harlequin and Woman with Necklace* (p. 42), painted by the artist in Rome in 1917 and acquired by the Musée National d'Art Moderne in 1965.

Between 1980 and 1983, the work of Matisse served the couturier as a regular reference point. Yves Saint Laurent admired the painter's audacious use of colour, his bold harmonies and his love of ornament, and discreet allusions to Matisse first appeared in his work in the early 1970s. He shared Matisse's sense of the East as a 'revelation', readily admitting that after visiting Morocco he too had become 'more sensitive to the light and the colours and most particularly noticed the light *on* the colours'.[8] The year after the Matisse exhibition at the Musée National d'Art Moderne, with works drawn from the museum's own collections,[9] Yves Saint Laurent's Autumn–Winter 1981–82 collection included skirts adorned with motifs inspired by the artist's large-format gouache cut-outs. In 1981, in a particularly heartfelt homage to Matisse, he created a faithful replica of the traditional peasant blouse in *The Romanian Blouse* (pp. 56–57), which Matisse gave to the museum in 1953.

Pierre Bonnard, Sonia Delaunay and Fernand Léger also became regular sources of inspiration. Léger's late compositions inspired an evening gown with a dark velvet bodice and a skirt embroidered with satin and taffeta appliqué (p. 59). The colourful assortment of plant motifs adorning the lower skirt recalls Léger's *Polychrome Flower* (1952; p. 58), created in collaboration with the ceramicist Roland Brice and acquired by the museum in 1954.

The Spring–Summer 1988 collection – which the couturier called his 'Homage to Artists' – featured capes (p. 38) whose Cubist designs recalled the major exhibition devoted to Georges Braque's collage work by the Musée National d'Art Moderne six years earlier.[10] One of the pieces in the collection was, in fact, directly inspired by *Aria de Bach* (painted in 1913 and housed in

5. *Rhinoceros* by Xavier Veilhan, being moved out of the
Saint Laurent Rive Gauche boutique, 1999.

Washington's National Gallery of Art). Alongside the capes, other designs recalled Braque's *Birds* from the 1950s, with oversized embroidered motifs by François Lesage extending well beyond the model's natural silhouette. Yves Saint Laurent had hitherto confined himself to discreet allusions to or direct transpositions of modern art; what he did now was to transform his runway show into a series of paintings brought to life.

Fashion was not a focus of the Musée National d'Art Moderne and the museum was slow to represent Yves Saint Laurent himself. It was not until 1988 that it acquired a portrait of the couturier for its photography collection – a nude shot (p. 22) taken by Jeanloup Sieff as part of the ad campaign for the couture house's first perfume for men. Published in *Vogue Paris* in November 1971, this rather Christ-like image had the conservative press up in arms. Yet it had been Yves Saint Laurent himself who had said 'I want to shock. I want to pose nude.'[11] Portraits of many of his predecessors in the world of haute couture, acquired by the museum in the 1990s, sat alongside this photograph: Cristóbal Balenciaga, Coco Chanel, Jacques Doucet, Jacques Heim, Jeanne Lanvin, Elsa Schiaparelli and Jean-Charles Worth,[12] photographed by Laure Albin-Guillot, Richard Avedon, Dora Maar and Man Ray.

In December 2000, Xavier Veilhan's *Rhinoceros*, commissioned by Pierre Bergé and Hedi Slimane for the Rive Gauche store in New York, was acquired for its collections by the Centre Pompidou. Although the artist denied any such inspiration,[13] this sculpture – which contrasts a lumbering, prehistoric-looking creature with a bold red carapace that resembles the chassis of a racing car – definitely echoes the admiration felt by Yves Saint Laurent and Pierre Bergé for the rhinoceros drinks cabinet designed by Claude Lalanne in 1966. The year that the museum acquired Veilhan's *Rhinoceros* was also the year in which Yves Saint Laurent, Pierre Bergé and the Maison Yves Saint Laurent made a substantial donation 'for the purposes of renovating the permanent exhibition rooms and improving the display conditions of the modern collections', following a three-year closure of the museum. As early as 1993, the pair's sponsorship had helped the museum to acquire *Blue I* (1961), the final painting in a triptych by Joan Miró that the Centre Pompidou had taken almost a decade to acquire in its entirety. Following Yves Saint Laurent's death, Pierre Bergé kept up this generous sponsorship tradition by contributing significantly to the acquisition of Giorgio De Chirico's *The Revenant* (1918), pre-empted by the State at the sale of the Saint Laurent–Bergé collection in 2009. The painting, selected by André Breton for the 'First Exhibition of Surrealist Painting' at Galerie Pierre in November 1925, represented an important landmark in the artist's oeuvre and had previously belonged to another couturier-collector, Jacques Doucet.

The couturier demonstrated his lasting connection to the museum in January 2002, on the occasion of his farewell show (fig. 4). To both Yves Saint Laurent and Pierre Bergé, the choice of the Centre Pompidou as a venue was an obvious one, serving as evidence of the extent the Yves Saint Laurent had, over the years, continued to keep 'one foot in couture and the other in the Musée d'Art Moderne'.

1. Piet Mondrian, 'Le Home, la Rue, la Cité', *Vouloir*, no. 25, 1927.
2. Piet Mondrian and Michel Seuphor, *Tableau-poème: textuel*, 1928/1956.
3. Quoted by Germain Viatte in *L'Envers de la médaille. Mondrian, Dubuffet: les pouvoirs publics et l'opinion*, Strasbourg: L'Atelier contemporain, 2021, p. 154.
4. A second painting by Mondrian, *New York City* (1942), would be acquired by the museum nine years later, in 1984.
5. Yves Saint Laurent, *Yves Saint Laurent par Yves Saint Laurent*, Paris: Herscher/Musée des Arts de la Mode, 1986, p. 213.
6. Jean-Jacques Lévêque, 'Vasarely, le partage des forms', *Arts Loisirs*, no. 74, 1967, p. 185.
7. Yves Saint Laurent quoted in Suzy Menkes, Jéromine Savignon, Olivier Flaviano et al., *Yves Saint Laurent Haute Couture: Catwalk*, London: Thames & Hudson, 2019, p. 272.
8. Interview with Yvonne Baby, 'Yves Saint Laurent au Metropolitan de New York. Portrait de l'artiste', *Le Monde*, 8 December 1983.
9. 'Matisse dans la collection du musée', Paris, Centre Pompidou/Musée National d'Art Moderne, 14 November 1979–13 January 1980.
10. 'Georges Braque. Les papiers collés', Paris, Centre Pompidou/Musée National d'Art Moderne, 17 June–27 September 1982.
11. Laurence Benaïm, *Yves Saint Laurent*, Paris: Grasset, 2018 (new edition), pp. 355–358.
12. The portrait of Jean-Charles Worth in this collection, photographed by Man Ray, is also a nude.
13. See 'Le *Rhinocéros* de Xavier Veilhan', *Connaissance des arts*, April 2010, p. 81.

Centre Pompidou

Works exhibited

Pablo Picasso, *The Violin*, 1914, oil on canvas, Centre Pompidou.
Yves Saint Laurent, 'Homage to Georges Braque' cape, Spring–Summer 1988,
wool embroidered with sequins, beads and buckskin.

At the runway show for Yves Saint Laurent's Spring–Summer 1988 haute couture collection, thirteen embroidered 'Cubist capes'[1] heralded the arrival of the 'Dove' wedding dress, the culmination of the whole show. Loosely inspired by actual works, these capes seemed to the public to be 'paintings by Braque, Miró, Gris, recreated as if by magic'.[2] The embroidered cape pictured here is a direct reference to Georges Braque's collage *Aria de Bach* (1913, National Gallery of Art, Washington DC), which was included in the exhibition of collages by Braque at the Centre Pompidou in 1982.[3] The monochrome shades – greys, blues, ochres – are enlivened by the use of embroidery that reflects the light. Yves Saint Laurent thus turns an assemblage of everyday objects, a still life, into something animated by the movements of the model, with the intention, in his words, of setting 'static things in motion on the body of a woman.'[4]

Yves Saint Laurent owned several Cubist works, including *Compotier, quotidien du Midi* (1912–13) by Georges Braque and *Musical Instruments on a Table* (1914–15) by Pablo Picasso, and drew considerable inspiration from Dora Vallier's catalogue raisonné of Braque's prints, published four years earlier.[5] He particularly admired the 'softer'[6] form of Cubism that succeeded its rigorously analytical counterpart. Picasso's *The Violin* – shown above – typifies this return to colour and textural contrasts. Skilfully juxtaposing simulated collage elements, figurative motifs and tiny dabs of colour, Picasso has produced a vibrant, almost musical, composition that contrasts with the austerity of earlier Cubist works.

A.C.-S. & M.S.

1. Programme for the runway show for the Spring–Summer 1988 haute couture collection.
2. Katherine Pancol, 'En quelques mois, il a reconquis un royaume qui éblouit le monde entier', *Paris Match*, 12 February 1988.
3. 'Georges Braque: les papiers collés', Paris: Centre Georges Pompidou, Musée National d'Art Moderne, 17 June –27 September 1982.
4. Patrick Thévenon, 'Le choc Saint Laurent – Dans le match de la mode, il sort une arme secrète: le Cubisme', *Paris Match*, 12 February 1988.
5. *Ibid*.
6. Yves Saint Laurent quoted in Suzy Menkes, Jéromine Savignon, Olivier Flaviano et al., *Yves Saint Laurent Haute Couture: Catwalk*, London: Thames & Hudson, 2019, p. 272.

Pablo Picasso, *Harlequin and Woman with Necklace*, 1917, oil on canvas, Centre Pompidou.
Yves Saint Laurent, 'Homage to Pablo Picasso' dress, Autumn–Winter 1979–80,
black and white satin crepe.

In 1917, Picasso worked on the costumes and sets for Serge Diaghilev's ballet *Parade*, then, two years later, on those for *Le Tricorne* (1919). His painting, to which he transposed the monumentality and themes of these ballet sets, was profoundly marked by the experience. *Harlequin and Woman with Necklace* is typical of this decorative shift: the economical use of colour, the flatness of forms and construction, together with the imposing format, were all new elements taking the painter's art in the direction of the 'return to order' of late 1917. The figure of the Harlequin became a central motif in Picasso's work during this period, taking the role of the artist's alter ego.

While Yves Saint Laurent may well have known this painting, bequeathed to the Musée National d'Art Moderne by Eva Gebhard, Baroness Gourgaud, in 1965, it was the discovery of Picasso's costume designs, when these were presented to the Bibliothèque Nationale in 1979, that really influenced the couturier's collection of the same year. This crepe evening ensemble, for example, was inspired by Picasso's Harlequin costume for *Le Tricorne*. 'My collection is based on that specific moment and constructed like a ballet. [...] I worked with blocks of colour, like a painter. [...] I saw the side panels made the hips disappear. It turned into a very practical style.'[1]

Several exploratory sketches, as well as multiple designs shown on the runway, reveal the couturier experimenting with two-colour contrasts – in particular, black and white – with alternating panels of fabric creating a geometric effect. Like Picasso, Yves Saint Laurent was always interested in the theatre and theatrical costumes, to the point that he thought long and hard about joining the world of entertainment before opting definitively for fashion. A.S. & M.S.

1   Yves Saint Laurent, interview with Bernadine Morris, *New York Times*, 4 August 1979.

Reconstruction of the wall of André Breton's studio, 42 rue Fontaine, 1922–66, Centre Pompidou.
Yves Saint Laurent, coat, Spring–Summer 1967, raffia with macramé collar
embroidered with wooden beads.

Pierre Bergé and André Breton were very briefly acquainted in 1949, when they were both members of the pacifist movement Citoyens du Monde, founded by Garry Davis. Pierre Bergé was at the time editor of the short-lived journal *La Patrie Mondiale*, which had the backing of the Surrealists. At a later date, Bergé acquired the only handwritten manuscript of Breton's autobiographical novel, *Nadja* (1927–28).[1]

In 1960, when he and Yves Saint Laurent acquired the first work for their art collection, a large Senufo bird, from the Galerie Charles Ratton, Bergé must have been reminded of his visits to Breton's atelier-apartment in the rue Fontaine. Breton owned a small Dogon statuette and Pierre Bergé and Yves Saint Laurent acquired several of these small highly stylized sculptures.

In 1967, Yves Saint Laurent showed a Spring–Summer haute couture collection inspired by African art. These creations were also contemporaneous with a retrospective of Pablo Picasso's work that set out to re-evaluate the artist's relationship with African art.[2] The coat, made from russet raffia with a macramé collar incorporating wooden beads, appears to be directly inspired by traditional costumes worn by the Dogon people in their ritual dances – images of which Yves Saint Laurent could have seen in his copy of Jacques Maquet's book *Civilisations noires*.[3]

A.C.-S. & M.S.

1. 'La bibliothèque de Pierre Bergé', first sale (Sotheby's),
   11 December 2015, lot no. 166.
2. 'Hommage à Pablo Picasso', Paris: Grand Palais, Bibliothèque
   Nationale, Petit Palais, 18 November 1966–12 February 1967.
3. Published in 1966 by Éditions Marabout (first published
   under the title *Afrique, les civilisations noires* by Horizons
   de France in 1962).

Alberto Giacometti, *Man and Woman*, 1928-29, bronze, Centre Pompidou.
Yves Saint Laurent, gown, Spring–Summer 1967, organza with rhodoid and wooden beads.

The Spring–Summer 1967 haute couture collection, known as the 'Bambara' collection, included a long black gown with cone-shaped breast ornaments that shimmered like a beetle's shell. Saint Laurent described it as 'a dress made for showing only', adding that it 'would be ridiculous to think of it as a "dress for wearing". [...] The fabric is a type of plastic made to look like wood. It's a totem.'[1]

Made of organza embroidered with rhodoid and wooden beads in a geometric repeat motif, the dress is inspired by a handmade Malian cotton fabric known as bogolan. Several dresses in the collection use similar combinations of unusual materials, playing a role in the contemporary bid to put African art on the map, an initiative in which the exhibition 'L'Art nègre. Sources, évolution, Expansion', held in Dakar, and then Paris, in 1966, was especially instrumental. 'Africa contains treasures, both creative and imaginative,' the couturier said. 'And working with African culture has been a source of fascination and enrichment for me.'[2]

This exceptional piece is somewhat reminiscent of the Surrealist sculptures of Alberto Giacometti, in particular his *Man and Woman* (1928–29), embodying a similar nervous tension between eroticism and menace. Pierre Bergé and Yves Saint Laurent acquired several pieces of furniture designed by Giacometti for the interior designer Jean-Michel Frank. In the article he devoted to the sculptor in *Documents*,[3] Michel Leiris sees this piece as reflecting 'true fetishism', defined as 'the love of – really *being in love with* – ourselves, projected outwards and clothed in a solid carapace that imprisons it between the limits of a precise thing, such as a piece of furniture which we can use, in that vast and strange room we call space'.[4] Several years later, we see this same apparent 'petrification'[5] of desire at work in Yves Saint Laurent's designs.

A.C.-S. & M.S.

1. Yves Saint Laurent quoted in 'Pierre Dumayet met Saint Laurent sur le gril', *Elle* (France), 23 March 1967, p. 120.
2. Yves Saint Laurent in *Yves Saint Laurent. Dialogue avec l'art*, exh. cat., Paris: Fondation Pierre Bergé–Yves Saint Laurent, 10 March–31 October 2004.
3. Michel Leiris, 'Alberto Giacometti', *Documents*, no. 4, September 1929.
4. *Ibid*.
5. *Ibid*.

Robert Delaunay, *Rhythm, Joie de Vivre*, 1930, oil on canvas, Centre Pompidou.
Yves Saint Laurent, 'Homage to Pablo Picasso' dress, Autumn–Winter 1979,
moiré faille with satin and faille appliqué decoration, satin belt.

When he visited the exhibition 'Diaghilev: les Ballets russes', held at the Bibliothèque Nationale in 1979,[1] Yves Saint Laurent saw the costumes Picasso had designed for the ballet *Parade* in 1917. They made a huge impression on him and he went on to produce his own interpretation of the outfit worn by Léonide Massine, in the role of a Chinese conjuror.[2] 'I was inspired by a costume Picasso did for Diaghilev's ballet *Parade*. Picasso used three colours, black, yellow and orange. I did the appliqués in many colours,'[3] explained the couturier, who had used this particular technique since his early years. It was a modern kind of embroidery that enabled him to interpret a painting in the form of embroidered patches of overlapping colour. By comparing the motif created by Yves Saint Laurent with Picasso's painting, we can clearly see how the couturier has adapted the lines and curves of the original to suit the surface of the fabric, a moiré silk satin by the Italian manufacturer Taroni. For the appliqué itself, he called upon the services of Andrée Brossin de Méré, one of the most brilliant practitioners of this technique, with whom he had collaborated since the 1960s.

Aside from the influence of Picasso, the dynamic motifs and blocks of solid colour are reminiscent of the work of Sonia and Robert Delaunay, much admired by the couturier, who had several books about these two artists in his library. From the early 1910s onwards, the couple were primarily interested in exploring colour and motion. 'The true new painting will begin when we understand that colour has a life of its own, that the infinite combinations of colour have their poetry and their poetic language,'[4] wrote Sonia Delaunay, adding that 'in this field, there are endless new possibilities'. She herself designed garments using a principle she called 'simultaneous contrasts', making geometric compositions from a patchwork of fabric remnants.   A.S. & M.S.

1. 'Diaghilev: les Ballets russes', Paris: Bibliothèque Nationale, 17 May–29 July 1979 (exhibition held to coincide with the 50th anniversary of the death of Diaghilev).
2. *Léonide Massine, le prestidigitateur chinois*, stage photograph, no. 222 in the exhibition catalogue.
3. Yves Saint Laurent, interview with Bernadine Morris, *New York Times*, 4 August 1979.
4. Sonia Delaunay, *Nous irons jusqu'au soleil*, Paris: Robert Laffont, 1978, p. 169.

Piet Mondrian, *Composition in Red, Blue and White II*, 1937, oil on canvas, Centre Pompidou.
Yves Saint Laurent, *Homage to Piet Mondrian* dress, Autumn-Winter 1965-66,
wool jersey in cream, black, red, yellow and blue.

In early July 1965, Yves Saint Laurent had already designed a great many garments for his coming collection when he realized that nothing was sufficiently modern for his taste, with the exception of a dress whose embroidered motif was taken from a painting by Serge Poliakoff. With this in mind, the couturier began to seek new inspiration for his collection – and found it in Michel Seuphor's book *Piet Mondrian, Life and Work* (1956), the only biography of the Dutch artist in print at the time. The very next day, the entire couture house (183 employees, including 120 seamstresses spread across six workshops[1]) started work on the new designs.

On 6 August 1965, a week later than his fellow couturiers, Yves Saint Laurent was ready to show 106 designs, more than twenty-five of them inspired by Mondrian's paintings. This warm tribute to the artist marked a key moment in the history of fashion – the moment when, for the first time, fashion forged links with modern art. In order to create a dress that was a 'manifesto of sorts',[2] the couturier appropriated the artist's work, transforming a two-dimensional painting into a three-dimensional garment that combined the boldness and purity of its source of inspiration. Yves Saint Laurent explained this revolutionary choice as a fierce desire to begin creating dresses made up of colours rather than lines. Fashion needed to move, to become fluid: the 'Mondrian' dresses were designed to be 'brilliant and perpetually in motion like coloured mobiles'.[3]

The Mondrian dress was so successful that it spawned a host of imitations, especially in the United States. This phenomenon, which was both immediate and global, may have done a great deal to boost the couturier's reputation, but it also introduced the work of Mondrian – previously unrepresented in French museums – to a wider audience. However, it was not until 1969, four years after Yves Saint Laurent designed his Mondrian dresses, that the Musée de l'Orangerie held the first retrospective of the Dutch artist's work.

A.C.-S

1. 'Yves Saint-Laurent s'explique: "J'en avais assez de faire des robes tristes pour milliardaires blasées!"', *Le Journal du dimanche*, 15 August 1965.
2. Bernard Blistène, 'Une œuvre d'art peut-elle en cacher une autre?', interview by Farid Chenoune, in *Yves Saint Laurent*, exh. cat., Paris: Petit Palais, 11 March–29 August 2010, Paris: Éditions de La Martinière, 2010.
3. Patrick Thévenon, 'Yves Saint Laurent invente les robes "mobiles". Le couturier qui a pensé aux femmes d'aujourd'hui', *Candide*, 15 August 1965.

Henri Matisse, *The Romanian Blouse*, 1940, oil on canvas, Centre Pompidou.
Yves Saint Laurent, ensemble inspired by Henri Matisse, Autumn–Winter 1981–82,
wool muslin blouse embroidered with sequins, beads and chenille;
velvet skirt; velvet and passementerie belt.

Of all the painters Yves Saint Laurent admired, Henri Matisse was the most important: 'For me, he is *the* painter. More so than Picasso, whose genius I don't dispute; but my love for Matisse, with his apparently peaceful life and the way he experiments with colour, is constant.'

The couturier's private collection included no fewer than four works by the artist – ranging from works of the 1910s (*The Cuckoos*, 1911) to the gouache cut-outs (*The Dancer*, 1937–38). And in his library, located in the studio at 5 avenue Marceau, he had around a dozen books devoted to Matisse, including a monograph whose cover depicts *The Romanian Blouse* (1940), a work donated to the Musée National d'Art Moderne by the artist in 1949.

From 1936 onwards, Matisse regularly dressed his models in Romanian blouses, traditional folk costumes embroidered with stylized motifs which his friend, Romanian artist Theodor Pallady, sent him from Bucharest. In the spring of 1940, after he had produced several versions of the painting, he completed this portrait of Lydia Delectorskaya wearing a loose blouse with full sleeves that fills the whole canvas. In 1981, Yves Saint Laurent reinterpreted the painting, proceeding gradually, like the artist himself, reworking, stylizing and refining the motifs: 'I have always wanted to create that blouse,' he said. 'I love traditional Eastern European costumes. They are cut very simply. A Romanian blouse is timeless. All these peasant costumes come down through the centuries without going out of fashion.'

L.F. & M.S.

Centre Pompidou

Fernand Léger, *Polychrome Flower*, 1952, cement and plaster, Centre Pompidou.
Yves Saint Laurent, 'Homage to Fernand Léger' gown, Autumn–Winter 1981–82,
black velvet bodice, white faille skirt with satin and taffeta appliqué.

Created for the Autumn–Winter 1981–82 haute couture collection, the 'Fernand Léger gown'[1] has a bodice and sleeves in black velvet and a contrasting skirt in white silk faille decorated around its lower half with appliqué fabric and repurposed embroidery swatches. The vibrancy of the colours and the profusion of varied and dynamic shapes give the dress a real sense of movement. The atelier worksheet for this design mentions 'large Fernand Léger flowers', referring to a theme dear to the artist at the end of his life. This 'painting in needlework',[2] or 'artist dress' as Yves Saint Laurent called it,[3] was the product of a close collaboration between the couturier and the embroiderer Andrée Brossin de Méré, whose work he described as the 'magic of a true artist'.[4]

Yves Saint Laurent and Pierre Bergé owned no fewer than six paintings by Fernand Léger. 'While classic in appearance, my tastes are very modern. My artistic reference points are Mondrian, Picasso, Fernand Léger...',[5] the couturier explained. Léger and Yves Saint Laurent also shared the same artistic sensibilities as collectors, since they were successive owners of a wooden sculpture by Constantin Brancusi, entitled *Madame L.R.*

A.C.-S.

1. Programme for the runway show for the Autumn–Winter 1981–82 collection.
2. *Textiles suisses*, 1 October 1981, p. 81.
3. *Le Nouvel Observateur*, 23 December 1983.
4. 'Die grosse alte Dame der Pariser Modewelt: Stoffkreateurin Andrée Brossin de Méré – Der Stoff, aus dem die Träume sind', *Annabelle*, 1 July 1981, p. 87.
5. Yves Saint Laurent, 'Mon destin, d'Oran à New York', *Paris Match*, 29 September 1994.

Jackson Pollock, *The Deep*, 1953, oil and enamel on canvas, Centre Pompidou.
Yves Saint Laurent, coat, 1984, white ostrich feathers with black-dyed tips, on silk organza.

Designed for the show *Hollywood Paradise* in 1984, this feather coat is among the striking costumes that Yves Saint Laurent made for Zizi Jeanmaire. Intended to be worn during her famous staircase routines – a landmark in the history of musical revues, a field revolutionized by the dancer and her husband, choreographer Roland Petit – its construction was a technical tour de force. The feathers were arranged to create a contrast between black and white and transformed the performer into a bird-like creature of the night, all delicacy and lightness. For the couturier, whom Jeanmaire first met in 1959 in the ateliers of Maison Dior, it was a formidable challenge that involved creating 'a sense of monumentality and a picture postcard feeling, at one and the same time'. 'The fact is', he continued, 'that musical cabaret, even more than theatre, is life turned on its head. Poor materials look rich and vice versa. Forget what's normal....'[1]

  Although Yves Saint Laurent never confirmed his source of inspiration, the milky white, airy texture of the coat is reminiscent of the paintings of Jackson Pollock, in particular his monumental *The Deep* (1953), a key piece in the retrospective of the American artist's work held at the Centre Pompidou in 1982. In around 1951, Pollock had gone as far as he could with his drip technique – which involved letting paint drip directly on to the canvas – and returned to the question of a painting's ground and surface. In *The Deep*, Pollock partially painted over a large black 'void' with white and little flecks of red, leaving space for imaginative interpretation and the resurgence of discernible forms. The vibrations of light that were a legacy of the 'all over' technique inevitably appealed to Yves Saint Laurent. When asked about their art collection, Pierre Bergé acknowledged the issue of potential gaps, saying: 'The main reason is that we bought the works we happened to come across. [...] We were never in the presence of a Rothko, or a Bacon or a Barnett Newman or a Pollock, although these are people we greatly admired.'[2]

L.F. & M.S.

1. Yves Saint Laurent, interview with Edmonde Charles-Roux, *Les Lettres Françaises*, 1972.

2. Pierre Bergé in 'Pierre Bergé: "Il ne faut jamais se comporter en propriétaire avec les œuvres d'art"', *L'Express*, 19 February 2009.

Martial Raysse, *Made in Japan – La Grande Odalisque*, 1964, acrylic paint, glass, plastic fly
and synthetic fibre braid on photograph mounted on canvas, Centre Pompidou.
Yves Saint Laurent, coat, Spring–Summer 1971, green fox fur.

The Spring–Summer 1971 collection, christened the 'Liberation' or 'Scandal' collection, marked the end of the futuristic visions of the 1960s and opened the way for the retro spirit of the 1970s, an era tinged with an aura of daring. The padded shoulders, puff sleeves and platform heels, the short wraparound dresses with plunging V-necks and the heavy makeup were all aesthetic references to Paris in the 1940s, under the German Occupation.

Responding to the unusually harsh criticism that this show received, Yves Saint Laurent declared: 'I prefer to shock rather than to bore through repetition.'[1] And, as it happened, retro fashion rapidly took over the high street, a great many designers drew inspiration from it, and New York was soon to announce that 'Old is in!'[2]

A key piece in the collection, this fox-fur coat, worn over a black silk jersey body and teamed with high-heeled strappy shoes, has echoes of *Les Dames du bois de Boulogne* (1945), directed by Robert Bresson, which was one of Yves Saint Laurent's favourite films. Taking his inspiration from the costumes worn by the 'women of easy virtue', like the cabaret dancer played in the film by Élina Labourdette, Yves Saint Laurent came up with a striking look that was entirely at odds with bourgeois conventions. The colour green – which had long been a colour overlooked by fashion – recalls the unearthly shade that Martial Raysse used to rework icons of art in his 'Made in Japan' series, created between 1963 and 1965 – here the green exaggerates the kitsch element of artistic appropriation. Photographed, cropped, spray-painted, then adorned with trinkets and a plastic fly in a final act of desecration, Jean-Auguste-Dominique Ingres's masterpiece *La Grande Odalisque* (1814, Musée du Louvre) is turned into a symbol of mass consumption of cheap goods: 'Beauty is bad taste,' Martial Raysse said. 'You have to push fakery as far as it will go. Bad taste is the dream of beauty that is trying too hard.'[3]

L.F. & M.S.

1. Yves Saint Laurent quoted in *Elle* (France), 1 March 1971.
2. See Fiona Levis, *Yves Saint Laurent. L'homme couleur de temps*, Monaco & Paris: Éditions du Rocher, 2008, p. 132.
3. Jean-Jacques Lévêque, interview with Martial Raysse, *Gazette des Beaux-arts*, no. 21, 1962.

Martial Raysse, *America America*, 1964, neon and painted metal, Centre Pompidou.
Yves Saint Laurent, 'Homage to Pop art' dress, Autumn–Winter 1966–67,
wool jersey in green, pink and navy.

These cocktail dresses in jersey, 'the only modern fabric'[1] according to Yves Saint Laurent, were first shown to the public in August 1966.

Jigsaws of colour and fabric, these short dresses owe a great deak to the spirit of Pop art, a movement familiar to Yves Saint Laurent via the work regularly shown at the Galerie Sonnabend and Galerie Iolas in Paris.[2] While design no. 85 (see p. 81) recalls works by Roy Lichtenstein, notably *Sunrise* (1965) with its sun, dune and sea motifs,[3] the dress pictured opposite echoes the heart motif that was regularly used by Jim Dine. The scooped and slightly waved necklines add to the sense of movement, while the bright, acid colours bring to mind the works of the Nouveaux Réalistes, such as Raymond Hains and Martial Raysse. Yves Saint Laurent met the latter at the Théâtre des Champs-Élysées, when he attended the premiere of Roland Petit's ballet *L'Éloge de la folie*, for which Raysse designed the costumes. The French artist had already come to the attention of American Pop artists, most notably Andy Warhol, via the 'Dylaby' exhibition at Amsterdam's Stedelijk Museum in 1962, and a second exhibition at the Iolas Gallery in New York in 1964. At the New York exhibition, Raysse showed *America America*, a monumental neon sculpture recreating a detail of the Statue of Liberty. As the artist himself explained, 'With neon, you can project the idea of colour in motion, that is to say, a movement of sensibility, without agitation.' It was a concept that was likely to appeal to Saint Laurent, whose own ideas about movement and colour were very similar.

The runway show for this haute couture collection, the tenth under Yves Saint Laurent's own name, held in the salons at 30 bis rue Spontini, was attended by the Nouveaux Réalistes Jean Tinguely and Niki de Saint Phalle – the latter a Maison Saint Laurent client herself; one of her *Nana* sculptures was installed in the courtyard of the first Saint Laurent Rive Gauche boutique in the rue de Tournon.

A.C.-S. & M.S.

1. *Life*, 2 September 1966 (half the designs for Yves Saint Laurent's Autumn–Winter 1966–67 collection were made of jersey).
2. See *Women's Wear Daily*, 1 August 1966.
3. See *Tages Anzeiger Magazin*, 20 December 1975, p. 20.

Centre Pompidou

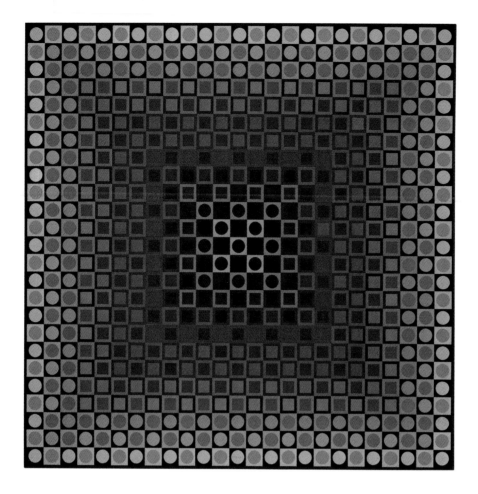

Victor Vasarely, *Alom (Dream)*, 1966, collage on plywood, Centre Pompidou.
Yves Saint Laurent, dress, Autumn–Winter 1968–69, wool muslin with geometric print
in brown, orange and blue. [p. 70] Jumpsuit, Spring–Summer 1970, black silk crepe
with geometric print in ivory and brown. [p. 71] Dress, Spring–Summer 1969,
black silk crepe with orange and white dot print.

These three haute couture designs, which were shown, respectively, in the 1968, 1969 and 1970 collections, are made of print fabrics by Maison Abraham, a Swiss firm based in Zurich and Lyons. Yves Saint Laurent had collaborated closely with Abraham since the founding of his couture house, and the firm's director, Gustav Zumsteg, was one of his close friends. Himself a collector of modern art, Zumsteg paid particular attention to the motifs of his fabrics, which were frequently inspired by works of art he had discovered while thumbing through numerous reference works. In his view, 'modern art is an inexhaustible source of inspiration... an essential aid.'[1]

The geometric motifs of these three ensembles explicitly reference the world of Op art, notably the works of Victor Vasarely. In the early 1960s, the artist expressed the desire to create a shared 'planetary' language. To this end, he developed a system of 'plastic unity' based on the concept of modules: 'circular cores are die-cut [...] from coloured squares. The shape and the background are independent of one another. The red oval cut from a red square can be inserted into a green square.' Vasarely's visual vocabulary expanded way beyond his own art, invading the world of popular culture and fashion magazines.[2] '"Planetary folklore" has now been born,'[3] the critic Michel Ragon said a few years later. Yves Saint Laurent would have seen works by Vasarely in the apartment of his friends Betty and François Catroux. Decorated in an 'Op' style, the apartment had been the subject of an article in *Vogue* entitled 'Op-art-ment'.[4]   A.C.-S. & M.S.

1. Gustav Zumsteg quoted in Christian Geelhaar, 'Mode – Kunst – Mode: Gespräche mit Yves Saint Laurent und Gustav Zumsteg', *Tages Anzeiger Magazin*, 20 December 1975, p. 23.
2. Victor Vasarely quoted by S. Gokalp in *Collection art graphique – La collection du Centre Pompidou, Musée national d'art moderne*, ed. Agnès de la Beaumelle, Paris: Centre Pompidou, 2008, p. 360.
3. Michel Ragon, foreword to the exhibition catalogue *Vasarely, polychromies multidimensionnelles*, Paris: Galerie Denise René, 1970.
4. 'Op-art-ment: A Contemporary Shell Masking Seventeeth-century Bones – The Paris Apartment of M. and Mme François Catroux', *Vogue US*, 15 February 1970.

Centre Pompidou

Ellsworth Kelly, *Black White*, 1988, oil on canvas, Centre Pompidou.
Yves Saint Laurent, full-length evening gown, Autumn–Winter 1965–66, black silk crepe.

Yves Saint Laurent and American artist Ellsworth Kelly shared an admiration for Henri Matisse, as well as for Piet Mondrian, Constantin Brancusi and Claude Monet. Their working practices, while each bound by distinct formal constraints, showed close similarities. In 1949, while he was a student in France, Kelly created his first works dealing with colour and its relationship to surrounding space. *Black White* (1988) reflects the artist's continuing preoccupation with the autonomy of colour and form. The two adjoining panels, one black and one white, are separated by a diagonal and held in a state of tension, neither able to unbalance the other. Kelly explained that if he had created the same image on a single canvas, the line of separation between the two would be painted and one of the colours would dominate the other.

Within this dialogue that demonstrates not only the close connections but also the differences between the two artists, it is interesting to note Kelly's interest in textiles. In 1951, his visual experiments attracted the attention of the fabric manufacturer Gustav Zumsteg – who was to become one of Yves Saint Laurent's regular suppliers – and Kelly subsequently produced some designs for Zumsteg. A year later, in Sanary-sur-Mer, Kelly designed a dress made of monochrome panels, which he described as 'a way of getting colour off the wall and having it walk around the room',[1] and which summed up, in essence, his approach to space. The couturier took a similar approach, announcing in 1965: 'I suddenly understood that dresses were no longer to be composed of lines but of colours. I understood [...] that we should regard [them] as a mobile.'[2] This crepe dress designed for the Autumn–Winter 1965–66 collection is a perfect example: minimalist in its structure, it looks as if it has simply been cut from the colour black.   M.M. & M.S.

1. This dress with its abstract motif was designed in 1952 for Kelly's friend Anne Weber. She made the dress from Kelly's design, but it has since disappeared. In 2013, Kelly recreated the dress, a version of which is now housed in the Metropolitan Museum of Art.
2. Yves Saint Laurent quoted in *Candide*, 15 August 1965.

Gary Hume, *The Moon*, 2009, gloss paint on aluminium panel, Centre Pompidou.
Yves Saint Laurent, 'Homage to Tom Wesselmann', Autumn–Winter 1966–67,
wool jersey in purple, black and pink.

Shown as part of the Autumn–Winter 1966–67 haute couture collection, this evening dress is made from panels of wool jersey by Maison Racine, in three colours: the silhouette of a figure in pink on a violet ground, while the back of the dress is plain black. The subject represented becomes the object: a nude female body, whose arm moves when the wearer's arm moves, clothes the body of a real-life woman. Despite the complex technique, the dress itself is simple and uncontrived. The motif is the garment's only dynamic element. This female nude, like the face in profile that adorns a cocktail dress in the same collection, is a direct reference to the 'Great American Nudes' series painted by the American Pop artist Tom Wesselmann.[1]

Featured on the cover of *Life* magazine in September 1966 (see p. 26), the dress was photographed by Jean-Claude Sauer – along with others from the same Pop-inspired collection that were illustrated inside the magazine – in front of a monumental book of matches by Raymond Hains. At around the same time, the work of Hains, a member of the Nouveaux Réalistes, was shown at the Galerie Iris Clert in Paris, at an exhibition entitled 'Seita et Saffa: copyright by Raymond Hains'. The dynamic and brightly coloured images in *Life* showed the modernity and imaginative flair of Yves Saint Laurent's designs – a form of 'Pop' fashion that was to prove surprisingly durable. Since the early 1990s, the artist Gary Hume, a member of the group known as the Young British Artists, has produced work using iconography, colours and techniques – such as the use of household gloss paint – that are strongly influenced by Pop art. Like Wesselmann's cut-outs and reappropriations – the very works that had appealed to Saint Laurent – Gary Hume's paintings take a playful approach to isolated anatomical details; *The Moon* (2009) features the image of a girl's arm reaching up, holding aloft a large yellow pompom.

A.C.-S. & M.S.

1. See Christian Geelhaar, 'Mode – Kunst – Mode: Gespräche mit Yves Saint Laurent und Gustav Zumsteg', *Tages Anzeiger Magazin*, 20 December 1975, p. 20.

Etel Adnan, *Untitled*, 2010, oil on canvas, Centre Pompidou.
Yves Saint Laurent, 'Homage to Pop Art' dress, Autumn–Winter 1966–67,
wool jersey with appliqué in blue, navy, yellow and orange.

'The earth is as blue as an orange.'[1] Perhaps that line of poetry written by Paul Éluard in 1929, the most famous line in his *L'Amour la poésie*, goes some way to illustrate the connection between the work of Etel Adnan and Yves Saint Laurent, despite their apparent distance. Despite their profound differences, both of them enjoy the same elemental, often hedonistic and always highly sensitive relationship with colour.

In 1966, the couturier created dresses made of jersey whose blocks of colour, arranged in jigsaw-like fashion, evoked brilliant landscapes loosely inspired by North American art. 'There was a beach with a sun like in the works of Roy Lichtenstein: with the dunes and the sea and a big yellow sun. In turquoise blue',[2] Yves Saint Laurent said.

The work of Etel Adnan reflects the world's intangible beauty. In this series, produced in 2010, the artist paints interior landscapes that draw on her memories of real places, ranging from Mount Tamalpais in California to the coastline of Lebanon. It is a continuation of a way of thinking, both poetic and pictorial, that Adnan has pursued since the 1970s, one which abolishes any distinction between abstraction and figuration. With an astonishing economy of means, she paints a mountain, a patch of green and a blue sea, in a way that recalls the first lines of the epic poem 'The Arab Apocalypse', which the artist wrote in 1989.   M.M. & M.S.

1. First line of the poem of the same name, taken from the collection *L'Amour la poésie* (1929).

2. Yves Saint Laurent quoted in *Tages Anzeiger Magazin*, 20 December 1975, p. 20.

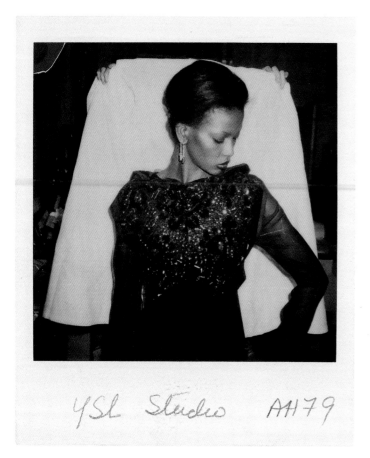

YSL Studio AH79

64   3125   PE80

Selection of Polaroids taken by couture house staff,
1979–2002, Musée Yves Saint Laurent Paris.

A great many artists (Robert Mapplethorpe, David Hockney and, in particular, Andy Warhol) have been fascinated by Polaroid cameras and this interest quite naturally extended to Yves Saint Laurent himself. The first time that the couture house used photographs was for the Spring–Summer 1979 show, although it was not until a year later that they became a standard part of preparations for a collection, and remained so until 2002. These snapshots were taken by staff from Maison Yves Saint Laurent, once a garment was nearing completion, the aim being to record the selection of accessories before a collection show. Each photograph was a working document. Attached to it would be the name of the model who would wear the garment, the name of the collection, the number of the worksheet and the position in the show's running order. It represented the final stage in the dressing process and enabled Yves Saint Laurent and Loulou de La Falaise to check each design before its wearer stepped on to the runway.

Taken in different areas of the building (changing rooms, salons, corridors, studio), these candid snapshots create an impression of bustling, joyous activity. In a number of the images, the garments are not yet finished or a member of the team appears unexpectedly in a corner, looking as if they are right at the creative heart of things.

The Musée Yves Saint Laurent Paris houses more than five thousand of these photographs, together with the cameras that were used to take the last of them.   A.C.-S

5076

AH 80 7h

1059

1 PE81

1109

55 PE81

2010 144

AH 81

3023   32
PE82

1125   76
AH82

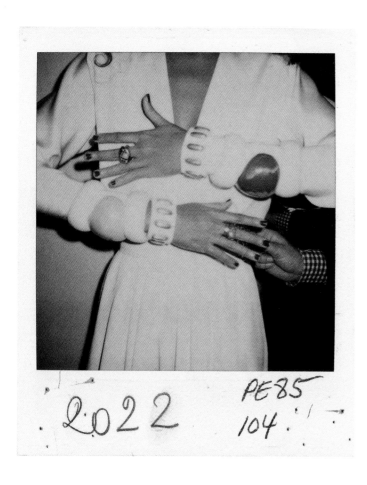

2022   PE85
104

57 Violeta 2211
AH85

Beverley (mariée)
133
2549 AH85

Khadija
98
2469
PE86

2630
123 AH86

Kirat LØ95
64 AH87

6207   40
        AH 93

6322 Nagali 59
           PE 94

6416 Nagali 34
     AH 94

6783 Magdalena 27
        AH 95

6759 Violeta 32 AH 95

7004 · Christelle 40 AH 96

7042² Stella/Alice PE 97

7137 Diana 6 AH 97

'Matisse really influenced
me with colour, since when
I started out, I only believed
in black. It took me a long
time to get used to colour.
Now I think I handle
colour brilliantly.'
Yves Saint Laurent

Yves Saint Laurent at the Musée d'Art Moderne de Paris

Fabrice Hergott and Charlotte Barat

[p. 90] Andy Warhol, *Portraits of Yves Saint Laurent*, 1972, screenprinting
ink and polymer paint on canvas, Musée Yves Saint Laurent Paris.

By incorporating Yves Saint Laurent's designs into its collections, the Musée d'Art Moderne de Paris (MAM) is showcasing the work of a near neighbour: the *hôtel particulier* at 5 avenue Marceau was a mere stone's throw from the museum. Yves Saint Laurent moved his haute couture house there in 1974, thirteen years after the MAM collections were installed in their current home, a masterpiece of Art Deco architecture, which had transformed the district when it was built in 1937.

The permanent collections of the Musée d'Art Moderne de Paris are located on the lower ground floor, while Raoul Dufy's vast mural, *La Fée Électricité*, has an entire room to itself. Yves Saint Laurent was constantly inspired by visual artists, acquiring many artworks and assembling an impressive library of art books and catalogues, which he consulted and annotated with a view to designing new creations of his own. He would often cross the avenue du Président-Wilson to admire the museum's colonnades and the works on display, immersing himself in the paintings of Sonia and Robert Delaunay, Henri Matisse and Pierre Bonnard. His couture designs demonstrate how intensely he scrutinized these works, which represented a sort of dream world of form and colour. Establishing a dialogue between Yves Saint Laurent's designs and the MAM's permanent collections is a question of recreating his literal and intellectual journeys back and forth – as if we were erecting a bridge between these two neighbouring institutions, two worlds utterly dedicated to art.

There will be those who wonder about the relevance of linking the world of fashion and the visual arts, since they are generally treated as quite separate spheres. What we should remember, however, is that while Yves Saint Laurent's interest in painting is intrinsic to his work, a great many artists, conversely, have also embraced the applied arts, seeing in them a source of creative inspiration with the potential to reach a wide audience. Raoul Dufy, for example, worked with Paul Poiret and later designed hundreds of fabrics for the textile firm Bianchini-Férier, while Sonia Delaunay produced 'simultaneous' coats, pyjama suits and swimwear. The history of the museum itself

1. Cocktail dress worn by Danielle Luquet de Saint Germain, Spring–Summer 1969, salons of 30 bis rue Spontini, Paris, 1969, photograph by Gunnar Larsen.

2. Anny Duperey dressed by Yves Saint Laurent for the film *Stavisky* by Alain Resnais, 1974. Sketch by Yves Saint Laurent and photograph by Peter Knapp, fashion shoot published in *Elle* (France), 25 March 1974.

reflects this permeability between different fields of creative endeavour: what is now the Salle Matisse housed for many years the Musée du Costume – the forerunner of the Musée Galliera, which did not open its doors until 1977 – and more recently, in 2013, the same room held the final display in the Azzedine Alaïa retrospective. It is also worth remembering that the MAM's decorative arts collection is a cornerstone of its identity. Founded in 1937, at the time of the Paris International Exhibition and the museum's inauguration, the collection features jewelry, objets d'art and furniture contemporaneous with the building's architecture. The museum remains faithful to this multi-disciplinary tradition and is still receptive to all forms of creativity, not only in the collections on display – which enable visitors to appreciate the whole breadth of creative endeavour – but also in its exhibitions, such as the recent show 'Les Flammes', dedicated to ceramics.

       Displayed in an Art Deco setting (p. 112), Yves Saint Laurent's film costumes help to evoke the sumptuous style of that era: the 1930s-inspired dresses he designed for the film *Stavisky* are surrounded by paintings, furniture and objets d'art from the same period, in surroundings not unlike the couturier's private residence. Saint Laurent himself was passionate about Art Deco – a passion that even filtered into his references to the unusual city-scapes of Giorgio De Chirico's paintings. Seeing the couturier's creations and the MAM collections side by side enables cross-referencing between disciplines while at the same time allowing a fresh look at each: the result is enriching in both directions. It was never the case that Yves Saint Laurent literally transformed a painting into a dress: 'I didn't copy them – who would venture to do that?' he said, talking of the artists who inspired him. 'I wanted to weave connections between the painting and the clothes, since I believe that a painter is always of our time and can be part of the life of each and every one of us.' Thus, in the 1980s, Yves Saint Laurent drew on Matisse's paper cut-outs (p. 111), adapting the technique to the world of fabrics and giving it an added three-dimensional quality – a process not dissimilar to cutting a toile, an essential stage in the making of a garment, as the collections of the Fondation Yves Saint Laurent demonstrate. Pierre Bonnard was also an inspi-ration; a set of designs of the early 2000s (pp. 117–119) replicated Bonnard's

3. Sketch and evening gown worn by Anna Pawlowski,
Autumn–Winter 1975–76.

delicate palette, bringing his glowing colour harmonies back to life almost fifty years after the artist's death.

While admiring many of the key practitioners of modernism, Yves Saint Laurent also maintained a dialogue with artists of his own generation: in addition to retrospective homages, this exhibition brings together some of the couturier's creations with artworks that are strictly contemporaneous with them. The selection of pieces either prefiguring or taken from the couturier's early ready-to-wear collections reflects the rise of consumerism in the 1960s, drawing a parallel with artists such as Daniel Buren (p. 142) and Alain Jacquet (p.128), who at that time were exploring the concepts of multiples and mass production in art.

The layout of the MAM Paris exhibition allows the museum's exhibits and the couturier's designs to 'talk' to one another in various ways, ranging from respectful homage to tacit sharing of a similar spirit or shared concerns. Yves Saint Laurent was attempting to emulate rather than imitate and these diverse sources of inspiration encouraged him to undertake his own bold experiments. From this infinitely rich storehouse of forms and colours, as well as fabrics, that vary spectacularly from one influence to another, he derived hundreds of designs, in a neverending process of creative renewal. It is this eclecticism, in the best sense of the word, that perhaps strikes us most forcibly. The insatiable curiosity that is the hallmark of Yves Saint Laurent's approach, along with his passion for very different fields of artistic endeavour, generate designs that are extraordinarily varied, from the strong, clean lines of creations inspired by Matisse to the brilliantly coloured, flowing ensembles that greet visitors to the Salle Dufy (p. 120). There are no constraints: Yves Saint Laurent switches freely between one artist and another, and invites us today, in the same spirit, to accompany him on this joyous, vibrant journey of rediscovery of the great names of modernism.

Musée d'Art Moderne de Paris

Works exhibited

Henri Matisse, *The Unfinished Dance*, 1931, three panels, oil and charcoal on canvas,
Centre Pompidou and MAM Paris.
Yves Saint Laurent, ensemble inspired by Henri Matisse, Autumn–Winter 1984–85, loose
'domino' coat in graduated shades of pale blue faille and black velvet; skirt in pearl satin.

For his Autumn–Winter 1984–85 haute couture collection, Yves Saint Laurent offered his own interpretation of the domino, a style of long hooded cloak once worn at masked balls. While retaining the
fullness of the garment, he removed the hood so that the woman wearing it would be proudly visible
in all her elegance. The alternating fabrics gave the garment a rhythmic interest, the black velvet
absorbing light while the blue faille reflected it. The range of blues and the wavy movement of the
black bands, which were fixed to the faille using appliqué embroidery by Andrée Brossin de Méré,
created an extraordinary feeling of dynamism.

     During the collection show, the model, Rebecca Ayoko, emphasized the theatricality of
this evening ensemble by spinning around to make the domino 'dance'. Norman Parkinson also
helped to immortalize the garment, photographing the model Iman wearing it in front of the Arc de
Triomphe du Carrousel, the fabric unfurling like an outspread wing as she raises her arms to heaven.

     As well as being an adaptation of Matisse's cut-out technique, the domino echoed Henri
Matisse's compositions in other ways too, notably the two versions of *The Dance* housed in the
Musée d'Art Moderne de Paris. The rhythmic repetition of the black bands and the combination of
restraint and dynamism in the garment's design are reminiscent of the artist's monumental paintings, as well as his restricted palette and formal economy. Likewise, the sheer energy required for
the garment to achieve its full impact recalls the energy and ardour of Matisse's dancers, whose
bodies spill out of the frame, their movements implicitly extending beyond the painted panels. A
similar sense of monumentality and power can be found in Yves Saint Laurent's domino, with the
spectacular sight of the garment flowing in three dimensions mirroring the heroic vibrancy of
Matisse's imagery.
C.B. & D.É.

Henri Matisse, *The Dance*, 1931–33, three panels, oil on canvas, MAM Paris.
Yves Saint Laurent, ensemble inspired by Henri Matisse, Autumn–Winter 1981–82,
bolero and top in black velvet; patchwork skirt in white moiré with black stripes.

The works of Henri Matisse are among those that have most inspired Yves Saint Laurent, sometimes directly – such as when he reproduced *The Romanian Blouse* in 1981 (pp. 56–57) – but often in a freer, more allusive fashion. Saint Laurent was fascinated by the painter's experiments with colour, but equally admiring of his paper cut-outs, the technique to which Matisse devoted the final years of his life, to the exclusion of almost everything else. Matisse was, as he himself put it, 'drawing with scissors' and 'cutting directly into colour' in order to create a variety of shapes which he then arranged into dynamic, lively compositions.[1] This 'new means of expression' enabled him to achieve a level of 'precision' that was unprecedented: 'Instead of drawing the outline and filling in the colour – the one modifying the other – I draw directly in colour,'[2] he explained.

The black and white dresses in the Autumn–Winter 1981–82 and Spring–Summer 1982 collections testify to Yves Saint Laurent's admiration for Matisse's paper cut-outs, transposing the artist's technique to the field of textiles. Created in collaboration with the fabric manufacturer Andrée Brossin de Méré, the skirts are decorated with abstract shapes that have been cut from a variety of materials and then fixed to a different-coloured ground using blanket-stitch appliqué, creating a relief effect. In 1982 – at a time when the influence of Matisse was most evident in the couturier's creations – Yves Saint Laurent and Pierre Bergé acquired a collage by the artist, one of his preparatory studies for Léonide Massine's ballet *Rouge et noir*. Dated 1938 and entitled *The Dancer*, the work uses the artist's paper cut-out technique to evoke the theme of dance, pursuing an experiment begun seven years earlier with the monumental series *The Dance,* now housed in the Musée d'Art Moderne de Paris. Well before the cut-out technique became his favourite means of expression, Matisse had created this immense mural using sheets of paper that he painted first before cutting them up and pinning them to the canvas, moving them around and modifying them as often as he felt necessary before arriving at his final composition. C.B. & D.É.

1. See Henri Matisse, 'Jazz', in *Écrits et propos sur l'art*, Paris: Hermann, 1972, rev. ed. 1992, p. 237.

2. Henri Matisse, 'Propos rapportés par André Lejard', in *Écrits et propos sur l'art*, Paris: Hermann, 1972, rev. ed. 1992, p. 243.

Musée d'Art Moderne de Paris

[Rear wall] Jean Dunand, *Sports*, decorative panels designed
for the smoking room of the SS *Normandie*, 1935, MAM Paris.
Yves Saint Laurent, costumes designed for Anny Duperey in *Stavisky* by Alain Resnais, 1974.
[Opposite] Coat in cream raw silk and pleated gown in cream silk crepe.
[p. 114] Cardigan in ivory wool; polo shirt in ivory and navy wool; skirt in ivory wool muslin.
[p. 115] Jacket and skirt in black wool crepe; blouse in black chiffon.

Yves Saint Laurent was fascinated by the cinema and designed costumes for a number of films. His collaborations were often the result of a particularly close connection with a director or star, as is clear from these words by Alain Resnais, who asked him to design Anny Duperey's outfits for the film *Stavisky* in the early 1970s: 'Yves Saint Laurent is the opposite of a costume supplier. He is a full member of the creative team. What I found most striking was that he doesn't just design costumes for the scene in which they are slated to appear but sees them as part of a dramatic continuity.'[1]

In *Stavisky*, Anny Duperey plays the wife of the eponymous hero, a financier and embezzler arrested for fraud whose murder, in 1934, sent shockwaves throughout France. Yves Saint Laurent designed eight outfits for the actress, who said that it was as if they had been 'cut and almost sewn on to me', adding: 'I slip into them as if I were slipping into the skin of the character.'[2] This restrained but elegant wardrobe was directly inspired by Yves Saint Laurent's passion for the 1930s. An avid collector, throughout his life he would carry on acquiring Art Deco furniture and objects, including two large vases made by Jean Dunand that were among his very first purchases. His decorative art collection had many similarities with the collection held in the Musée d'Art Moderne de Paris, which includes a host of objets d'art and furniture sets, some of which were acquired at the time of the Paris International Exhibition of 1937. Ranging from the elegant furniture made by Jacques-Émile Ruhlmann and Eugène Printz from a range of precious materials, to Jean Després's geometric jewelry, and Maurice Marinot's gorgeous glassware, the collection housed in the MAM Paris perfectly reflects the peak of Art Deco style when cabinetmakers, gold- and silver-smiths, glass artists and sculptors were vying with one another to produce ever more sumptuous luxury articles for a well-heeled clientele. Jean Dunand's lacquer wall panels – originally intended for the first-class smoking room on the luxurious liner *Normandie* – are an embodiment, in monumental form, of that period of glorious ostentation and intense creativity which Yves Saint Laurent so admired.

C.B. & L.F.

1. *Yves Saint Laurent. Théâtre, cinéma, music-hall, ballet*, Paris: Fondation Pierre Bergé –Yves Saint Laurent, 2007, p. 43.

2. Anny Duperey, quoted in 'Anny Duperey dans *Stavisky*: C'est aussi l'affaire de Saint Laurent', *Elle*, 25 March 1974.

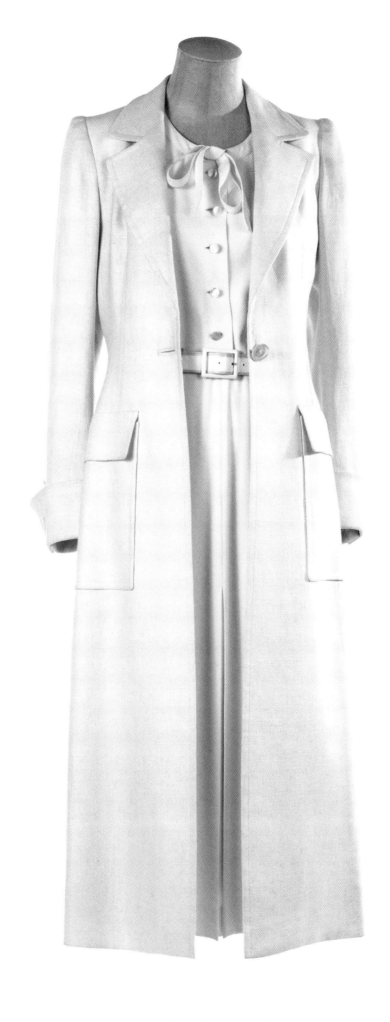

114   Musée d'Art Moderne de Paris

Musée d'Art Moderne de Paris

Pierre Bonnard, *The Garden*, c. 1936, oil on canvas, MAM Paris.
Yves Saint Laurent, ensembles inspired by Pierre Bonnard, Spring–Summer 2001.
[Opposite] Organza blouse with mauve and magenta print; organza skirt with pink,
violet and blue print. [p. 118] Organza blouse with red and orange print;
organza skirt with yellow, pink and orange print.

For his Spring–Summer 2001 collection, Yves Saint Laurent designed a series of dresses decorated with motifs inspired by the delicate and colourful palette of the painter Pierre Bonnard. More precisely, these creations with their floral tones reflect the couturier's admiration for the garden views painted by Bonnard in the 1930s, when the artist was living in Le Cannet, a stone's throw from the Mediterranean. The fabrics recall the profusion of flowers and riot of greenery present in paintings such as *The Garden*, the dresses becoming metaphorical gardens in their own right.

While Bonnard's paintings are frequently suffused with a vague sense of existential unease, Yves Saint Laurent primarily draws on the works' radiant serenity and colour harmonies. He replicates their harmonious colours, rejecting the use of contrast and choosing prints that marry similar rather than complementary colours. His dresses also echo the dense pictorial surfaces so typical of Bonnard, mirroring the complex and uninterrupted lattice of brushstrokes patiently applied by the artist. The line of the skirts, too, and the choice of organza create an impression of lightness that is very like the lightness Bonnard introduces into his paintings. The forms that Bonnard paints seem to have lost their weight and solidity; they seem almost to have dissolved and merged one with another. His canvases are like evocations of a waking dream, over which 'the eye wanders without a single impediment'.[1]

C.B. & L.F.

1. *Bonnard*, text by Jean Clair, Paris: H. Scrépel, 1975.

Musée d'Art Moderne de Paris

Raoul Dufy, *La Fée Électricité*, 1937, 250 panels, oil on plywood, MAM Paris.
Yves Saint Laurent, full-length evening ensembles, Autumn–Winter 1992–93.
[Opposite] Absinthe satin jacket and fuchsia satin gown.
[p. 122] Bronze satin jacket and emerald satin gown.
[p. 123] Buttercup satin jacket and green satin gown.

These three ensembles – each comprising a full-length gown and a paletot jacket in contrasting satins – make use of stunning, and radical, colour combinations. 'I like muted colours in the daytime [...] whereas in the evening I want women to be birds of paradise,' Yves Saint Laurent declared, and these three creations display a similarly vivid and radiant colour palette, their monochrome fabrics becoming wonderful foils for each other.

These experiments with colour are reminiscent of the work of Raoul Dufy, in particular the startlingly bright, pure colours the artist used for *La Fée Électricité*, a monumental mural created in 1937, depicting the story of the invention of electricity. Its two hundred and fifty wall panels, installed in the Musée d'Art Moderne de Paris since 1964, combine huge expanses of colour filled with figures and other narrative elements and a playful approach to colours and outlines that creates a dissociation between the two. The resulting effect of transparency was exactly what the artist was seeking to achieve, while the medium (a very light oil paint) created by the chemist Jacques Maroger enabled him to accentuate the near-watercolour effect and produce colours that were 'brilliant, ductile, transparent'.[1]

The airy lightness of Dufy's composition is replicated in Yves Saint Laurent's three designs, with the use of silk satin giving a marvellous sense of fluidity while creating shine and shimmer. Dufy too wanted his works to be a source of light, since, in his own words, 'without light, colour is lifeless'.[2] His canvases no doubt owe a great deal to his own experience with fabric design; in the early 1910s Dufy collaborated briefly with Paul Poiret before going on to work for almost twenty years for the Lyons-based silk manufacturers Bianchini-Férier (incidentally, also a regular supplier to the Maison Yves Saint Laurent), producing gouache and watercolour designs for hundreds of fabrics.

C.B. & L.F.

1. Raoul Dufy, 'Comment je comprends la peinture', *Beaux-Arts*, 27 December 1935.

2. Letter from Raoul Dufy to André Lhote, 1943, quoted in Martine Contensou, *La Fée Électricité*, Paris: Paris Musées, 2008, p. 50.

Lucio Fontana, *Neon Structure for the 9th Milan Triennale*,
1951, white neon tubing, HT power transformer, MAM Paris.
Yves Saint Laurent, paletot jacket, black velvet embroidered with silver 'dust',
Autumn–Winter 1983–84. [p. 126] Blouse in pearl grey satin, Autumn–Winter 1962–63.
[p. 127] Gown in silver grey panne velvet, Autumn–Winter 1975–76.

A combination of silk satin, panne velvet and silk velvet embroidered with glittering silver,[1] these three creations are all made of fabrics that create subtle light effects. Their silvery shades give them a glossy, metallic look, while the draping and gathering of the fabric increases the potential for shimmer and shine. All three pieces (taken from different collections) were designed to be worn at night, under artificial light – a more uneven and dramatic light source than daylight. Depending on the wearer's movements, they reflect the light in different ways, producing a fascinating range of visual effects.

The idea of light as a creative principle is a constant theme of Lucio Fontana's work, embodied in original and spectacular fashion in the neon sculpture that the Argentinian-Italian artist made in 1951 for the 9th Milan Triennale. Fontana argued in favour of a radical renewal of artistic techniques that would bring them up to date and put them in tune with the times. Neon – formerly used only for advertising signage – struck him as a particularly suitable medium, since it embodied a 'new element [...] that had found its way into the aesthetic of the man in the street'.[2] The year of its creation, his monumental *Neon Structure* loomed over the grand staircase at the Palazzo dell'Arte, illuminating the whole area, like an immense drawing in light suspended in the air. Made of a hundred metres of fluorescent tubing, this 'fantastic new decoration' soared overhead like a fabulous arabesque of light, marking 'the start of a new form of expression'.[3]

During the 1960s, a great many artists would adopt neon as a favoured medium. For his Autumn–Winter 1966–67 haute couture collection, Yves Saint Laurent himself designed a bridal gown in white velvet incorporating a neon light in the shape of an oversized lily – *lys* in French, an anagram of the couturier's initials. The model held the lamp as if it were a bouquet of flowers, its battery concealed inside her palm.[4]

C.B. & A.C.-S.

1. Programme for the Autumn–Winter 1983–84 couture collection.
2. Letter from Lucio Fontana to Gio Ponti, 30 July 1951, in *Lucio Fontana: lettere 1919–1968*, Milan: Skira, 1999.
3. *Ibid.*
4. 'Saint-Laurent's Collection Full of Surprises', *Cork Evening Echo*, 5 August 1966.

Alain Jacquet, *Le Déjeuner sur l'herbe*, 1964, diptych,
four-colour screenprint on canvas, MAM Paris.
Yves Saint Laurent, jacket, jacquard wool in white, blue and black, Spring–Summer 1966.
[p. 131] Pea coat, jacquard wool in navy and white, Spring–Summer 1966.
Dress, silk crepe in black, green and white, Spring–Summer 1969.
Jacket, jacquard wool in green and white, Spring–Summer 1966.

Laurent's Spring–Summer 1966 haute couture collection was described in the contemporary press as 'fashion that is colourful, youthful, vibrant and bold'.[1] Several pieces feature geometric repeat motifs – alternating triangles in different colours or tiled triangles creating a pattern of two-coloured squares. Thanks to the small size and density of the motifs, however, the eye does not immediately recognize them as separate units but reads the colours as if they were overlapping.

Less than two years earlier, the French artist Alain Jacquet had experimented with similar optical effects in his iconic *Le Déjeuner sur l'herbe*, in which he reinterpreted Édouard Manet's famous composition by transferring onto canvas a photograph he had taken of some friends copying the poses of the figures in the original scene. In Jacquet's image, the use of the screenprinting technique is made obvious: rather than using the very fine mesh that was standard in advertising at the time, Jacquet chose to make the mesh visible, by enlarging the black, red, yellow and blue dots that form the image. Seen close up, the work therefore becomes hard to read: 'The bigger the dots, the more the image disappears,' Jacquet explained. 'But it is always recognizable eventually. The viewer just has to get the right distance away to be able to read it.'[2]

Almost a hundred versions of Alain Jacquet's *Le Déjeuner sur l'herbe* were mechanically reproduced, each slightly different, deliberately flipping the quasi-religious obsession with unique works of art, 'the idea being to make a picture like a mass-produced car'.[3] With their simplified, smooth, modern lines, these designs by Yves Saint Laurent heralded his first ready-to-wear collection, which was launched in September 1966 at the Saint Laurent Rive Gauche boutique in the rue de Tournon. Using the same strategy as for his haute couture designs, he created prototype garments – but in this case for reproduction on an industrial scale.   C.B.

1. *Le Méridional – La France*, 5 February 1966.
2. 'Alain Jacquet: le chemin, la voie, la manière d'agir',
   interview with Sylvie Couderc, in *Alain Jacquet*.

Oeuvres de 1951 à 1998, exh. cat., Amiens: Musée de Picardie,
   21 March–17 May 1998, p. 74.
3. *Ibid*.

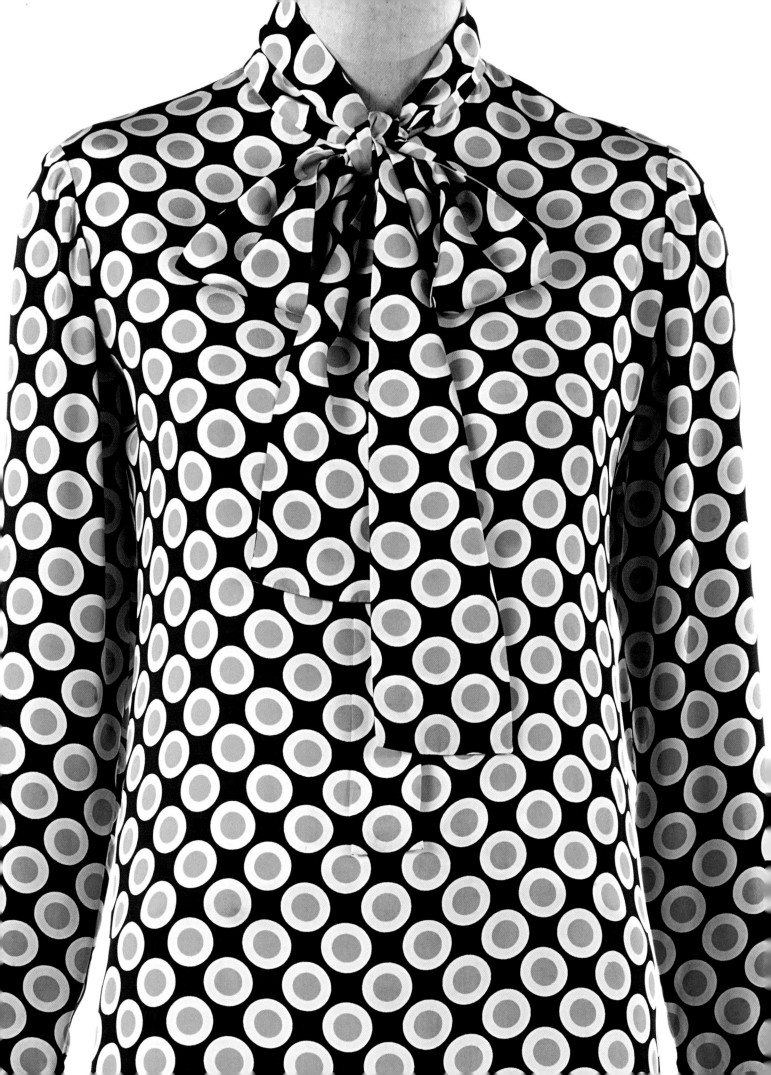

Giorgio De Chirico, *Idillio antico (Ancient Idyll)*, c. 1970, oil on canvas, MAM Paris.
Giorgio De Chirico, *Piazza d'Italia with Statue*, n.d., oil on canvas, MAM Paris.
Yves Saint Laurent, coat, black chenille wool with astrakhan effect, Autumn–Winter 1968–69.
[p. 137] Dress, silk crepe with marbled green print, Spring–Summer 1971.

Yves Saint Laurent's and Pierre Bergé's art collection included two paintings by the Italian artist Giorgio De Chirico. The mysterious motifs and unsettling atmosphere of De Chirico's paintings clearly made an impression on the couturier, since in addition to his costume and set designs for *The Two-Headed Eagle*, several of his ensembles are reminiscent of De Chirico's work.

The heavy fabric and sculptural form of this full-length coat in black chenille wool (Autumn–Winter 1968–69) create a solemn, statuesque quality that recalls De Chirico's compositions. Its rigid lines convey a similar sense of stillness and immobility to the one that emanates from De Chirico's paintings, especially those depicting huge and eerily deserted piazzas. Meanwhile, the astrakhan look of the velvety fabric, the black and gold buttons on the bodice and the black suede belt recall De Chirico's love of framing his pictures with rare or precious materials.

Similarly, the drapery of the silk crepe evening dress (Spring–Summer 1971 collection) recalls De Chirico's antique statues, while its marbled green colour evokes both the stonework of those statues and the painter's dominant palette of greens. With its camouflage-like print, this dress was an obvious fit for the couturier's 'Scandal' collection, first presented to the public on 29 January 1971. Inspired by the fashions of the 1940s, which by this time had found their way into flea markets, the collection harked back to the dark years of World War Two and the Occupation, another connection to the work of De Chirico: 'Artists [...] teach you to see things,' Pierre Bergé observed. 'De Chirico's oeuvre, like that of other artists, was like a premonition. And those big buildings with those arcades, those empty streets, show us what so-called fascist architecture, in Italy, would be like.'[1]

C.B.

1. Pierre Bergé and Laure Adler, *Pierre Bergé – Yves Saint Laurent. Histoire de notre collection de tableaux*, Arles: Actes Sud, 2009, pp. 44–46.

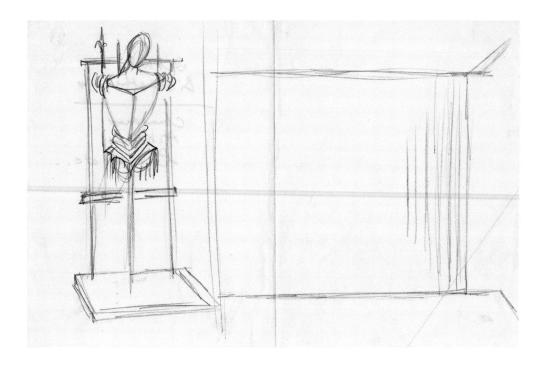

Yves Saint Laurent, set designs for the library in *The Two-Headed Eagle*
by Jean Cocteau, 1978, Musée Yves Saint Laurent Paris.

'It was my first theatre set. The hardest thing was forgetting the admirable images created by Cocteau and Bérard.'[1] Yves Saint Laurent was talking about *The Two-Headed Eagle*, a play by Jean Cocteau for which he designed costumes and sets when it played at the Théâtre de l'Athénée (with Jean-Pierre Dusseaux directing) from 4 February 1978. He was explaining what a challenge it had been, trying to ignore the designs Christian Bérard had come up with thirty-two years earlier for a production at the Théâtre Hébertot. Hundreds of preparatory sketches for *The Two-Headed Eagle* are conserved in the Musée Yves Saint Laurent Paris, and several of these – highly detailed and colourful pieces – are directly inspired by Bérard's creations, which the couturier first saw in Oran in 1946 and greatly admired. A second series of sketches is simpler and more austere and marks a change in Saint Laurent's vision for the play, prefiguring the final designs.

The three designs reproduced here come from this later series. One represents an overall view of the library (the set for Acts II and III) and the two others show details from the same set. The figures in the sketches have neither faces nor hair and are clearly influenced by the egg-headed mannequins that inhabit the compositions of Giorgio De Chirico, an Italian artist and forerunner of Surrealism, two of whose works – *The Anarchist's Bomb* (1914) and *The Revenant* (1917–18) – were owned by Yves Saint Laurent and Pierre Bergé. The figure in the latter painting – part-human and part-column – may have given Yves Saint Laurent the idea for his library-figure, whose body appears to be made of books. His sketch of a mannequin in armour, on the other hand, recalls the metal-clad figures in De Chirico's work. The stitches that hold their cloth heads in place are another detail that the couturier borrowed from these figures, while his backcloth with its geometric shapes, and the feeling of emptiness it conveys, can also be seen as referencing De Chirico's art, with its deserted squares and strangely foreboding atmosphere. De Chirico said of the mannequin that it is 'profoundly *non-living* and [that] this lack of life repels us, and makes it odious to us. Its appearance, at once human and monstrous, frightens us and frustrates us.'[2]

De Chirico himself was interested in the theatre and created his mannequin figures in the wake of Guillaume Apollinaire's plans to stage a play based on his own poem, 'Le musicien de Saint-Merry', in which a 'man without eyes or nose or ears' plays the flute. Alberto Savinio, De Chirico's brother, made several drawings of Apollinaire's faceless man, so giving the artist the idea for these motifs.[3]

C.B. & D.É.

1. Yves Saint Laurent quoted by Jean-Claude Loiseau in 'Points de mire', *Le Point*, no. 281, 6 February 1978.
2. Giorgio De Chirico, 'Discorso sullo spettacolo teatrale', *L'Illustrazione italiana*, 25 October 1942 (trans. Bianca Cerrina Feroni). Quoted in *Giorgio de Chirico. La fabrique des rêves*, exh. cat., Paris: Musée d'Art Moderne de la Ville de Paris, 13 February–24 May 2009, Paris: Paris Musées, 2009, p. 24.
3. See Willard Bohn, *Apollinaire and the Faceless Man: The Creation and Evolution of a Modern Motif*, Madison, NJ: Fairleigh Dickinson University Press, 1991.

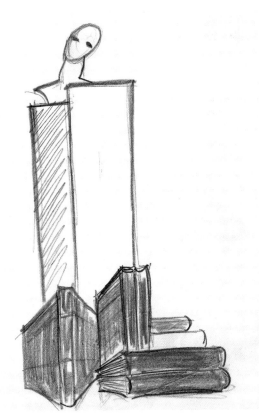

Daniel Buren, *Wall of Paintings*, 1995, acrylic paint on a set of 20 canvases, MAM Paris.
Yves Saint Laurent, denim coat dress, Saint Laurent Rive Gauche collection,
Spring–Summer 1970

On 26 September 1966, Yves Saint Laurent became the first couturier to open a ready-to-wear boutique under his own name. Located at 21 rue de Tournon in Paris, Saint Laurent Rive Gauche aimed
to be more accessible, more in tune with women's daily lives: 'Ready-to-wear is a gateway to everyday life,'[1] explained Yves Saint Laurent, championing 'a certain way of living, rather than a certain
way of dressing'. He was tired of working exclusively for 'jaded billionaires' and wanted to dress a
larger portion of the female population, announcing loud and clear: 'Down with the Ritz! Long live
the street!'

  He adopted a completely new approach, in terms of both the design of the garments and
the production and distribution chains. This newness was also reflected in the choice of fabrics: by
designing a coat dress in denim, Yves Saint Laurent was opting for a fabric which, as he saw it,
embodied modernity and the spirit of the times. 'Blue jeans', he said, 'are the perfect match between
a piece of clothing and an era.'

  During the 1960s, with the advent of mass consumption and the spectacular moderniza-
tion of Western lifestyles, the issue of the distinction between haute couture and ready-to-wear
found an echo in the field of the visual arts, where questions were being asked about the notions of
series, originals and multiples. The French conceptual artist Daniel Buren was exploring the idea of
'systematic repetition' in paintings that use the same unchanging 'visual tool' – in Buren's case,
alternating vertical stripes, in either white or a colour, each 8.7 centimetres wide. Rejecting the
notion of art being reserved for museums and galleries, the artist took over the street instead, applying his stripes to a varied range of supports before his works were destroyed.

C.B. & L.F.

1. See the filmed interview with Yves Saint Laurent at:
 https://museeyslparis.com/biographie/saint-laurent-rive-gauche

'My approach was
not to measure myself
against the greats,
but to try to learn lessons
from their genius.'
Yves Saint Laurent

Yves Saint Laurent's creations in the Gallery of Apollo

Anne Dion-Tenenbaum

[p. 144] Jacques Henri Lartigue, *Yves Saint Laurent*, 2 February 1976, silver print on coated paper, Musée Yves Saint Laurent Paris.

Thanks to the richness of their fabrics, and the skill and time that went into their making, the creations by Yves Saint Laurent displayed in the Musée du Louvre are the very embodiment of luxury. That these creations should be housed alongside the museum's sumptuous royal collections highlights the complex influences that fuelled the designer's imagination and the sheer extent of his curiosity. Indeed, they could hardly have found a more appropriate setting than the Gallery of Apollo, where Louis XIV's collection of hardstone vessels and some of the former crown jewels of France are displayed (fig. 1).

The Gallery of Apollo was designed by the architect Louis Le Vau and is situated on the first floor of the Petite Galerie – linking the old Louvre with the Grande Galerie – following the fire that destroyed the gallery's upper sections in 1661. Charles Le Brun worked on a design for the interior for Louis XIV between 1663 and 1677, envisaging paintings and sculptures revolving around the theme of the sun's movement through time and space, but his project was never completed. Several unfinished sections of the ceiling were filled in, during the 18th century, with reception pieces submitted to the Académie Royale de Peinture, but it fell to the architect Félix Duban to restore and complete the decor in 1849. Under his authority, the interior designer Charles Séchan coordinated the restoration of the cornice and panelling, bringing an opulence to the decor that was more characteristic of the 19th century than the age of Louis XIV. The central section of the ceiling was entrusted to Eugène Delacroix, who responded by painting his exuberant *Apollo Victorious over the Serpent Python*.

1. The Gallery of Apollo at the Musée du Louvre, designed by Louis Le Vau, 17th century.

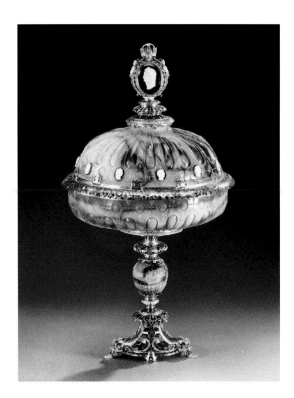
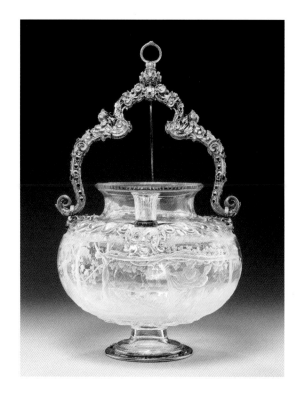

2. Covered round goblet, goblet 1300–1500, mount 1540–60, agate, ronde-bosse enamel on gold, sardonyx.
3. Vase, 16th century, rock crystal, enamel, gold and ruby.

Duban had intended that the gallery should remain empty, but in 1861 a decision was taken to house precious objects from the royal collections there. Since then, the 'gems' from Louis XIV's collection have been displayed in gilded wooden showcases in a neo-Louis XIV style, either in the centre of the gallery, along the walls or in glass-topped tables located in the window recesses. This collection, known as Louis XIV's '*gemmes*', brings together hardstone vessels carved by artisans from Ptolemaic Egypt up to the modern day, and from places ranging from Europe to China. These priceless objects have been fitted with gold and silver mounts, often long after they were made, in the Middle Ages, the Renaissance and the 17th century.

To these collections – placed in the gallery during the Second Empire – were added, during the Third Republic, the jewelled pieces reserved for the Musée du Louvre when the French crown jewels were sold in 1887. The jewels (including diamonds and other precious stones) were too closely associated with royalty in the eyes of the young Republic and were sold legally, but eight pieces were removed from the sale and passed to the Louvre, owing to their historical and artistic value. Other pieces were added to the collection as time went on, with the museum endeavouring, from the 1970s onwards, to buy back those jewels that had been sold.

Louis XIV displayed his collection of engraved hardstone objects – of which he was particularly fond – in his 'Cabinet of Rarities, Curiosities and Jewels' at Versailles, from 1682. They were arranged in low cabinets along with his medals, while the hardstone vases were placed on console tables against the mirror-lined walls. Yves Saint Laurent and Pierre Bergé also collected 'rarities' and displayed them in what could be described as a cabinet of curiosities, created for their rue de Babylone apartment by the interior designer Jacques Grange. This passion shared by monarch and couturier explains the many resonances between Yves Saint Laurent's creations and the objects on display in the Gallery of Apollo. The embroidery of the Maison Lesage, for example, brilliantly evokes the materials and decorative techniques, such as cameo work, that can be seen in the ornamentation of Louis XIV's hardstone vases.

4. Mirror, 1630–35, agate, rock crystal, gilding, ronde-bosse enamel on gold, emerald, garnet, brass, gold, ruby, sardonyx.

One such resonance can be found in Yves Saint Laurent's black velvet jacket, created in 1984, emblazoned with two large cameos on a red ground embroidered to look like jasper and set within a framework of scrolls, foliage and shells. There is a similarity here with the cameo-carved stones mounted on the lids of some of the vessels in Louis XIV's collection (probably as a way of highlighting these precious elements), in particular a covered cup made of agate whose lid is edged with portraits of the twelve Caesars and topped with a superb agate cameo, within an enamelled gold setting (fig. 3).

The jacket with gold and rock crystal embroidery (p. 165), which the couturier dubbed 'Homage to My House' and which was first worn in the runway show for the Spring–Summer 1990 haute couture collection, recalls the rock crystal vases that were among the most precious items of their kind in Louis XIV's collection. Rock crystal – a material strikingly similar in appearance to ice – has been a source of fascination since classical antiquity, as evidenced by Pliny the Elder in his *Natural History*. Lapidaries have treated this very hard stone in a playful fashion, creating a variety of forms – frames, shells, vases. Enamelled gold mounts, sometimes enriched with precious stones, serve as the perfect foil to highlight the crystalline clarity of the stone (fig. 2), and the Yves Saint Laurent jacket – a garment that appears to be literally smothered in crystal drops refracting the light – is similarly edged with a garland of gold leaves embroidered in relief.

To create the so-called 'Broken Mirror' jacket from the Autumn–Winter 1978–79 collection (p. 160), the couturier made playful use of another decorative element dating from the 17th century, by adorning the back of the garment with an embroidered *trompe-l'oeil* mirror, whose simulated cracks produce brilliant gleams of light. The gilding and sparkling effect are reminiscent of the rich decorations seen in the Gallery of Apollo, and also those in the Hall of Mirrors at Versailles, designed by the architect Jules Hardouin-Mansart to honour the Sun King. The mirror motif is reflected in the royal gemstone collection: in 1684, Louis XIV acquired a rock crystal mirror (fig. 4), framed with miniature columns and crowned with an indented pediment set with a

5. Frans Pourbus the Younger, *Marie de Médicis, Queen of France,*
first quarter of 17th century, oil on canvas.

cameo of a woman's head, the richness of the object enhanced with additional cameo work in sardonyx and garnet, emeralds, rubies and enamel.

Aside from their decorative motifs, all of these embroidered jackets draw on the tradition of court dress. In the 18th century, embroidery made use of gold (in reality, gilded silver) and silver thread, sequins, spangles, glass beads, precious and semi-precious stones, and even unusual materials such as fur, straw, feathers and insect wings. For the grandest occasions – such as audiences with foreign ambassadors and royal weddings – court costumes would be encrusted in precious stones. Writers and artists recorded the dazzling appearance of these glittering garments; one example is a portrait of Marie de' Médicis (fig. 5) by Frans Pourbus the Younger, showing the queen in a gown with slashed sleeves and a stomacher studded with gemstones and pearls. Doublets, and later jackets and waistcoats, were also adorned with precious stones. An inventory of the French crown jewels compiled in 1691 records three parures made for Louis XIV, the first in diamonds, the second in coloured gemstones and the third in pearls, which included buttons and boutonnières for jackets and waistcoats, as well as shoe buckles, hat pins and shoulder strap ornaments. During the Second Empire, some of the diamonds mounted as waistcoat buttons for Louis XIV were reset by the firm of Bapst into a 'reliquary' brooch for the Empress Eugénie (fig. 6). The two heart-shaped diamonds, positioned point to point, were bequeathed to his godson Louis XIV by Cardinal Mazarin, who was known to be fond of diamonds.

Musée du Louvre

In the 19th century, the tradition survived: Napoleon I, and later Louis XVIII and Charles X affirmed their power through the prestige of jewels. These gemstones, handed down from generation to generation until 1887, were reset to suit changing fashions and individual requirements, with the crown diamonds, notably, being mounted in official insignia, such as the cross, star and necklet of the Légion d'Honneur or those of older chivalric orders such as the Order of the Holy Spirit (fig. 7) and the Order of Saint Louis. Yves Saint Laurent's heart-shaped pendant (p. 157) would likewise accompany his designs throughout his career, reappearing in some new guise at every fashion show.

During the Second Empire, the Empress Eugénie, a woman renowned for her elegance, wore the crown jewels at official functions. However, whenever she left Paris for the country, the Regent Diamond, the 'jewel' of the whole collection, was probably replaced by a rock crystal copy for safety's sake. The art of imitating precious stones was not new. Rhinestones – a type of crystal with a high lead content that could convincingly be used to imitate diamonds and other gems – were invented by the jeweler Georges Frédéric Strass during the era of Louis XV; they became hugely popular and are still called 'strass' in French in their creator's honour. Yves Saint Laurent's 'Heart' pendant is a continuation of this particular tradition, being made of crystal, rhinestones and red glass.

6. Christophe-Frédéric Bapst, 'reliquary' brooch for the Empress Eugénie, 1855, diamonds, gold.
7. Insignia of the Order of the Holy Spirit, c. 1730, silver, diamond, gold, ruby.

Musée du Louvre

Works exhibited

'Heart' necklace worn by Victoire Doutreleau, Spring–Summer 1962,
salons du 30 bis rue Spontini, Paris.
Yves Saint Laurent, 'Heart' necklace, smoky grey rhinestones, red crystal cabochons, white
pearls and red glass pendant, designed in 1962 and recreated in 1979 by Maison Scemama.

The heart was one of Yves Saint Laurent's favourite motifs: 'I have been using the heart as a symbol
for a long time,' he said, 'variously reinventing it: as a powder compact, a piece of jewelry, a handbag.
In every colour: ruby, sapphire, emerald, amethyst, rock crystal. I have made dresses with it, and
scarves, and fabrics. The heart is here to stay.' Of all the many hearts he created, there is one that
is central to the history of the house: designed in 1962 and made by the Maison Scemama, Yves Saint
Laurent's 'Heart' necklace is iconic. It served as a kind of talisman and was included in every haute
couture and ready-to-wear collection show, worn by a model of the couturier's choice.
     This striking piece of jewelry symbolizes the height of luxury and yet, paradoxically, cocks
a snook at the conventions of *haute joaillerie*: instead of being made of precious stones, the necklace
is studded with rhinestones and crystal cabochons with a drop pendant in glass.   L.F.

'Broken Mirror' jacket, Autumn–Winter 1978–79, black velvet
embroidered with gold, silver and rhodoid.

This fitted jacket with padded shoulders is part of an evening ensemble in black Abraham velvet. Its apparent restraint is belied by the embroidered mirror on the back, created by the Maison Lesage, framed by gilded scrolls that continue round to the front of the jacket. The baroque-style mirror playfully combines a mixture of materials, being made of silver-coated plastic decorated with rows of stitches and tiny silver beads, and recalls the dazzling, gilded interiors of the 17th century, such as the Gallery of Apollo at the Louvre and, of course, the Hall of Mirrors at Versailles.

    Aside from its baroque decorative qualities, the mirror is also intended as a reference to the Surrealists, for whom the motif symbolized (among other things) a sense of the magical. Elsa Schiaparelli's 'Zodiac' collection of 1938 – also created with the assistance of the Maison Lesage – incorporated similar visual references. Yves Saint Laurent greatly admired Schiaparelli's 'witty flights of fancy'[1] and even wrote a foreword for a book about her work.[2] The magazine *Vogue Paris* beautifully grasped the couturier's vision for his Autumn–Winter 1978–79 collection when it wrote: 'With Saint Laurent, extravagance is always controlled, which is why his collection creates that impression of simplicity, ease, youthfulness and gaiety.'[3]

A.C.-S.

1. Yves Saint Laurent quoted in 'Yves Saint Laurent: je suis un homme scandaleux, finalement', *Globe*, January 1986.

2. Palmer White, *Elsa Schiaparelli: Empress of Paris Fashion*, New York: Rizzoli, 1986.
3. *Vogue Paris*, September 1978, p. 329.

Jacket, Spring–Summer 1980, black silk gazar with gold embroidery

This silk gazar jacket, part of an evening ensemble from the Spring–Summer 1980 collection, borrows decorative elements from the repertoire of South East Asian – specifically Burmese – dance and theatre. Its distinctive shape represents the flaming wings of divinities (*deva*) that are often depicted in paintings and sculptures, while also imitating the folds of the traditional draped Burmese garment known as a *longyi*. Originally used as court wear, from the 19th century onwards (after the British abolished the Burmese monarchy in 1885), the *longyi* was worn by actors playing royal, aristocratic or divine characters. Yves Saint Laurent's ensemble comprised a jacket, an over-jacket, sleeves and a collarette that were joined together to form a single garment. The appliqué technique used by the Maison Lesage for the silk organza leaves embroidered with gilded metal threads is similar to that used on Burmese costumes, which are often decorated using couching – a method of applying a mesh of gilded metal to the silk and stitching it in place.

     The jacket was worn by Diana Vreeland, whom the couturier described as 'one of the most exceptional people I ever had the chance to meet in my life', at a party he and Pierre Bergé hosted at the Paris Lido in 1982 to celebrate the couture house's 20th anniversary. A year later, Diana Vreeland organized an exhibition of Yves Saint Laurent's work at the Metropolitan Museum of Art in New York, the first museum show to be devoted to a living couturier. A.S.

Jacket, Autumn–Winter 1981–82, organza embroidered
with sequins, rhinestones and chenille.

This sublime jacket embroidered with gold and gemstones by the Maison Lesage is decorated with
a *boteh* or stylized palm leaf motif, best known as the paisley motif used on cashmere shawls. Saint
Laurent, incidentally, evokes the gorgeous gardens of Kashmir (a place he had never visited) in the
press kit for his fragrance Opium: 'I have drifted through Srinagar's beds of pink lotus gleaming in
the light of the full moon.' The complex embroidery of this garment, a combination of chenille and
facetted gemstones, and the use of rhinestone buttons, recall the jewelled costumes associated
with the India of the maharajahs – a concept the couturier had been experimenting with since his
first collection of Spring–Summer 1962. That same year, he created his famous 'Heart' necklace
(p. 157), in collaboration with the jeweller Roger Scemama. In shape, it was not unlike the *boteh* or
paisley motif, while its use of alternating stones recalled Mughal Indian jewelry. The couturier used
this stylized flower motif, either in appliqué form or as layered gold embroidery to create a relief
effect on a great many Asian-inspired designs, most notably in 1982 in his so-called 'Indian' collection. He also designed his own, more feminine, version of the *sarpech*, a turban ornament symbolizing
imperial power, and used it to adorn the turbans worn by some of the models in that show.

A.S.

'Homage to My House' jacket, Spring–Summer 1990, organza
embroidered with gold and rock crystal.

The Spring–Summer 1990 haute couture collection was conceived as a tribute, in 119 designs, to the talented women and men who had influenced Yves Saint Laurent or in some sense left their mark on him.[1] Closing the show was a 'Versailles jacket embroidered in gold and rock crystal',[2] given the name 'Homage to My House'.[3] The use of rock crystal reflected a centuries-old tradition of French luxury. Its resemblance to ice has been a source of fascination since classical antiquity and this precious material was featured in the collections of Louis XIV in the form of vases, now on display in the Gallery of Apollo at the Louvre.

Worn over a white silk satin dress, Yves Saint Laurent's jacket evokes 'the blue-greys of Paris reflected in the crystal chandelier in his office in the avenue Marceau',[4] explained the embroiderer François Lesage, to whom the couturier gave instructions: 'That reflection of sky and sun in the mirror, I would like that transformed into an evening dress.'[5]

While exemplifying the brilliance of haute couture, the embroidered jacket was also an expression of the love and gratitude that Yves Saint Laurent felt towards his couture house, and the women and men with whom he had worked for all those years. It was to them that he said: 'My children, my beauties, my wonders, my marvels, my beyond-talented ones, my loves, my queens, my kings and my princesses [...]. What a beautiful family we are. What love. What order, what determined pursuit of perfection. What self-respect... What a miracle.'[6]   A.C.-S.

1. *Yves Saint Laurent Haute Couture: Catwalk*, London: Thames & Hudson, 2019, p. 430.
2. Programme for the Spring–Summer 1990 couture collection.
3. Audio-visual archive for the Spring–Summer 1990 couture collection.
4. Laurence Benaïm, *Yves Saint Laurent*, Paris: Grasset, 2002 (revised edition), pp. 408–409.
5. Yves Saint Laurent, speech at the post-collection lunch, Paris, Hôtel de Crillon, 27 July 1988, quoted in Olivier Flaviano, '5 avenue Marceau, un lieu de mémoire(s)', in *Les Musées Yves Saint Laurent. Paris/Marrakech*, Paris: Éditions de la RMN-GP/ Musée Yves Saint Laurent, 2017, pp. 207–219.
6. *Ibid.*

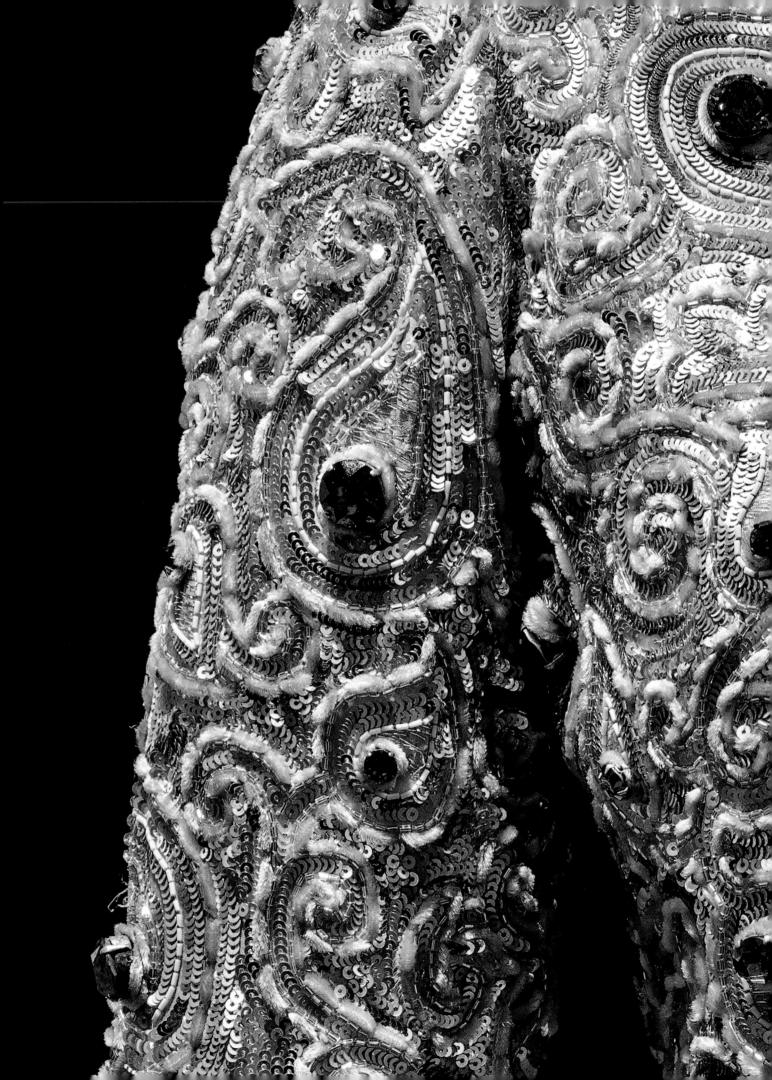

'Marcel Proust still
remains the greatest to me.
Proust is the one who said
the most about women and
whose life was a little like mine.'
Yves Saint Laurent

In the shadow
of Marcel Proust

Donatien Grau

[p. 170] Lord Snowdon, *Yves Saint Laurent*, 1980, Château Gabriel, Benerville-sur-Mer,
Normandy, chromogenic print, with kind permission of Frances von Hofmannsthal.

It would be no exaggeration to say that Marcel Proust was a constant presence throughout Yves Saint Laurent's life and work. 'He didn't read; only Proust,' remembered Pierre Bergé.

The story goes that, in 1954, the troubled adolescent – the same lad who three years earlier had drawn illustrations for *Madame Bovary* – began reading *À la recherche du temps perdu*. In 1956, at the age of twenty, he designed the costumes for a ball held by Alexis de Redé, christened the Bal des Têtes after the final section of *Le Temps retrouvé* (the seventh and final volume of *À la recherche*). In 1971, he devised the costumes for the Bal Proust, organized by Marie-Hélène de Rothschild at the Château de Ferrières to mark the centenary of the novelist's birth. In 1983, Pierre Bergé and Yves Saint Laurent acquired the Château Gabriel, in Benerville-sur-Mer – which was where Marcel Proust met the publisher Gaston Gallimard. They had the place decorated by Jacques Grange, with the emphasis on the Belle Époque style, and Yves Saint Laurent introduced references to Monet's *Waterlilies* that may well been a parallel with the work of the painter Elstir, a character in *À la recherche*, to whom the fictional town of Balbec in Normandy was a major source of inspiration. Each of the bedrooms in the château was given the name of a character in *À la recherche*. Yves Saint Laurent's own room was 'Charles Swann' – the pseudonym he used when he retreated there to escape the world, endeavouring to be a 'nobody' again. In 1990, in his 'Homages' collection, he showed two dresses inspired by Marcel Proust. And, in 2002, when he announced that he was leaving his couture house, his speech made reference to two writers: one was the poet Arthur Rimbaud – 'I rubbed shoulders with those that Rimbaud called "fire-makers"', he declared – and the other was Marcel Proust: 'Marcel Proust taught me that "the magnificent and pitiful family of the neurotic is the salt of the earth". Without knowing it, I was a member of that family.'

Beyond identifying a 'Proustian knot' for each decade, we may observe that Proust is connected to landmark moments in Saint Laurent's life and career. The dates alluded to above correspond to the designer's formative period; the year following his recruitment by Christian Dior on the recommendation of Michel de Brunhoff and preceding his appointment as artistic director of the house of Dior after the death of its founder; the year of his 'Scandal' collection that reworked the fashions of the 1940s; the year that New York's Metropolitan Museum of Art dedicated an exhibition to his work, the first of its kind dedicated to a living couturier; the year that he embraced sobriety – while at the same time producing a collection that was life-affirming; and, of course, the day of his departure from the firm. Proust influenced Yves Saint Laurent's entire trajectory throughout his life. Having established as much, it

Château Gabriel

Chambres		Invités
Guermantes	:	
Elstir	:	
Albertine	:	
Verdurin	:	
Saint Loup	:	
Morel	:	
Madeleine Lemaire	:	

Swann : Yves Saint Laurent
Charlus : Pierre Bergé

1. Bookplate for the Château Gabriel and guest list showing the rooms named after characters from *À la recherche du temps perdu*.

2. Auguste Renoir, *Portrait of Charles Le Coeur*, 1872, oil on canvas, Musée d'Orsay.

is important that we consider some of the reasons for that influence, what it meant for Yves Saint Laurent in practice, and how it may also have led to a moment of crisis.

The reasons may well be self-evident; primary among them is the dream of Paris as the centre of the world, something that Proust celebrated at the very moment that he recorded its ending – hence the enthusiasm for his work evinced by American writers such as Fitzgerald, Faulkner and Hemingway, who saw it as heralding Europe's demise, the dawn of a *translatio imperii* and the promise of American domination in the wake of the First World War. It is noteworthy, too, that in referring to both Rimbaud and Proust in the retirement speech he gave in 2002, Yves Saint Laurent was referencing one writer who had left Paris for Harar and another who had emphasized the city's – then waning – centrality. Saint Laurent lived and breathed Paris, and for him it never stopped being a focal point. Couture itself, both as an industry and as a focus of cultural exchange, also played its part in this. The costumes for the Bal des Têtes, designed by the young couturier who had recently returned from Africa, reflected just such a range of inspiration, bringing together diverse cultural influences under a Proustian umbrella. Almost fifty years prior to his farewell speech, as Yves Saint Laurent stood on the threshold of his career, the couturier was already feeling conflicted – torn between Rimbaud and Proust, the wider world and the heartland of Paris.

Proust celebrated a world that he knew had had its day but which, by celebrating it, he wanted to ensure would nevertheless live on. While he was a novelist very much in the great 19th-century tradition, Proust was also a practitioner of fictionalized autobiography, a genre he helped to modernize and, hence, to invent. Yves Saint Laurent, too, believed in couture, in café society, in the world of balls, like the Bal Proust organized by Alexis de Redé and Marie-Hélène de Rothschild, but he also knew that modern society was bound up with image (something he had mastered so well): that the fascinating, hidden lives of couture's privileged few, visible sometimes as mere shadows, now

Musée d'Orsay

3. Yves Saint Laurent, trouser suit worn by Esther Cañadas,
Spring–Summer 1999.

needed to be seen in the full light of day, where there was no longer any possibility of concealment. The success of couture itself meant opening up to a wider world: the result was his ready-to-wear line, Saint Laurent Rive Gauche.

It would be possible to argue that Yves Saint Laurent's championing of Proust helped to popularize the work of an author who was not as well known in 1951 as he is today. In the years following Proust's death, some of the aristocrats who had known him published memoirs describing the world in which they had lived. They knew that this world had come to an end and that Proust had captured its memory for posterity. In 1949, André Maurois published the biography *À la recherche de Marcel Proust*, for which he interviewed surviving witnesses. It was not until 1971, however, that a work of any substance was devoted to Proust's novel: Jean-Yves Tadié's *Proust et le roman*. Yves Saint Laurent recorded the transformations of his age, and the opening-up of Paris to other parts of the world, while simultaneously fostering the dream that was haute couture. In so doing, he made the Proustian world a reality. Emmanuel Levinas remarked that Proust's novel reflected the existence of a 'nobility without a Versailles'. The dresses in the 'Homages' collection – fresh, vibrant designs that would look perfectly at home today – established a link with the neo-18th century and the birth of haute couture – the era of Charles Frederick Worth – and the colours of Impressionism. And, talking of colours, few writers have described them quite as well as Marcel Proust.

Proust and his novel serve as a kind of double of Saint Laurent and his body of work: a cracked mirror in which the couturier sees himself. Proust and Saint Laurent have much in common: ultra-sensitivity, aestheticism, an appreciation, in terms of behaviour, of what is – and convention ordains should remain – invisible, being in the world and at the same time outside it, and of course queer identity, seen as a way of life not to be concealed but to be embraced, even by the upper echelons of society, the likes of Baron de Charlus in *À la recherche*. Yves Saint Laurent appears to have felt that he and Proust shared the same sensibilities. And there are the links with childhood too: Proust's famous questionnaire,

4. James Tissot, *The Circle of the Rue Royale*, 1868, oil on canvas

5. Yves Saint Laurent, trouser suit worn by Lavinia Birladeanu, Autumn–Winter 1998–99.
Trouser suit worn by Esther Cañadas, Spring–Summer 1999.
Ensemble worn by Diana Gaertner, Autumn–Winter 2000–1, photographs by Guy Marineau.

which Yves Saint answered before it became so well known, and the photograph he kept in his studio, depicting the novelist as a very young man.

We might well ask why Saint Laurent chose to call himself Charles Swann when he wished to divest himself of his own name. Rather than the creator of a great work, Charles Swann was merely a 'bachelor of art', the author of an essay on Maltese coins and a prefiguration of the novelist himself. Another passage from *À la recherche* comes to mind here. Referring to James Tissot's portrait *The Circle of the Rue Royale*, the narrator says: 'If in Tissot's picture representing the balcony of the Rue Royale club, where you appear with Galliffet, Edmond Polignac and Saint-Maurice, people are always drawing attention to you, it is because they know that there are some traces of you in the character of Swann.' Saint Laurent performed a similar alchemy for the wearer of his dresses. He was, at one and the same time, the narrator and Swann – the person of whom it cannot be said with any certainty whether he will ever produce a work of art, whether he really is an artist, or whether the work of art is in fact his life.

Saint Laurent's connection with Proust was largely subjective, but not exclusively so. Proust was one of the first French writers to put queer characters at the centre of his novel, and while paying homage to both men and women, he left the way open for a more indistinct, more fluid, and ultimately more creative, kind of identity. The description of the caresses lavished on Gilberte's body is a prime example – it is impossible to tell whether the body in question is male or female. This was a literary first, and it is not difficult to imagine what Yves Saint Laurent made of it.

The couturier never wanted to finish reading *À la recherche du temps perdu*. It was, he said, as if finishing the novel might bring him bad luck. There was no 'time regained' for Yves Saint Laurent, only the 'lost time' for which he searched tirelessly, and the great beauty of time lost with such elegance. He had therefore never read the section entitled *Le Bal des têtes*. He was following his own intuition, intuition that – even when the work in question was juvenilia – can be said to have somehow governed his career: the opening-up to the world, a fear of time taking everything away, the desire to produce a body of creative work and, simultaneously, an awareness that, as Cocteau said and as Baudelaire had written before him, fashion is the embodiment of transitoriness. There could be no resolution for Yves Saint Laurent, just as there could be no fiercer response to the ageing of that beautiful world he had known. The secret of this life lived in the shadow of Marcel Proust lies in the image of the eternal child, fascinated by beauty. The passage from *À la recherche* quoted by Yves Saint Laurent in 2002, and referred to above, is part of a tirade addressed by Doctor Cottard to the narrator's grandmother, and which therefore offers an external view of artistic sensibility. And yet, if we read further, we seem to hear the voice of Yves Saint Laurent himself: 'Everything great in the world comes from neurotics,' Cottard continues. 'They alone have founded our religions and composed our masterpieces. The world will never know all that it owes them, nor what they have suffered in order to bestow their gifts upon it.' Yves Saint Laurent was one of their kind – a neurotic who sought to make masterpieces while knowing that, as a couturier whose work was not made to last, he risked being merely a Charles Swann, a 'bachelor of art'. His works first found their way into a museum in 1983 and have been the focus of many exhibitions since, with no sign that the 2022 exhibition is likely to be the last. Events have continued to confirm the kinship with Proust that Yves Saint Laurent acknowledged in his farewell speech.

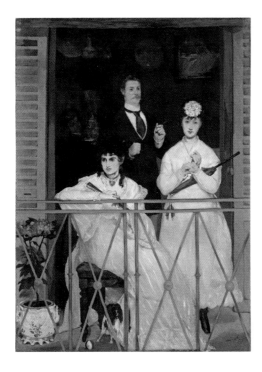 

6. Édouard Manet, *The Balcony*, c. 1868–69, oil on canvas.
7. Tuxedo worn by Kat Bespyatikh, Autumn–Winter 2001–2, photograph by Guy Marineau.

Musée d'Orsay

Works exhibited

[Opposite, left] Yves Saint Laurent, tuxedo, Autumn–Winter 1966–67, black grain de poudre and silk satin; blouse in white organdy. [Opposite, right] Tuxedo, Spring–Summer 1967, black wool gabardine; waistcoat and shirt in white cotton piqué.
[p. 184] Tuxedo, Spring–Summer 1967, navy alpaca; blouse in white organdy with plum satin bow.
[p. 185] Tuxedo, Autumn–Winter 2001–2, black velvet; blouse in white cotton.

It was in the late 19th century that the smoking jacket first appeared in England. Worn by men to protect their clothing from the smell of cigars when they retired to the smoking room, the jacket was soon accompanied by a pair of trousers and a white shirt. In the early 20th century, tuxedos (derived from smoking jackets) were widely adopted in place of tailcoats. Tuxedos typically comprised a jacket with silk satin lapels and trousers with a satin side stripe, accompanied by a white shirt and black bow tie.

For his Autumn–Winter 1966–67 collection, Yves Saint Laurent showed a female version of the tuxedo. It became a landmark in his career. The long, close-fitting jacket was worn with a jabot blouse, a black satin bow at the neck and high-heeled boots – a transgressive outfit designed as an alternative to an evening gown. The couturier continued to reinterpret the tuxedo over the next forty years, giving it padded shoulders, remaking it in velvet, as a dress, and in a version with no blouse worn underneath. As he said himself, 'Since 1966, when the first tuxedo appeared in my collection, the idea of women wearing men's clothing has continued to grow, develop, and establish itself as the very hallmark of the modern woman.' In experimenting with this dialectic, Yves Saint Laurent was reflecting the social changes of his age. In this, he was not unlike Proust, who brought out the feminine in men and the masculine in women, took pleasure in shifting, even inverting, gender identities and succeeded in exploring plurality in the subtlest of ways.   A.A. & D.É.

Musée d'Orsay

Yves Saint Laurent, gown designed for Marie-Hélène de Rothschild on the occasion
of the Bal Proust, 1971, ivory satin with ivory satin belt and bow.
[p. 189] Gown designed for Jane Birkin on the occasion of the Bal Proust, 1971
ivory crepe georgette and white lace with ivory satin belt and bow.

In order to celebrate the centenary of Marcel Proust's birth, Baron Guy de Rothschild and his wife Marie-Hélène decided to hold a sumptuous ball at the Château de Ferrières. The guests at the Bal Proust – held on 2 December 1971 – were immortalized by Cecil Beaton, who photographed them in Belle Époque costumes inspired by the characters in *À la recherche du temps perdu*, several of which were designed by Yves Saint Laurent.

The couturier adored Proust – in 1991, he said 'Proust is the one who said the most about women and whose life was a little like mine'[1] – and was delighted to accept the commission. Several of the gowns were made in his ateliers, including those worn by Baronne de Rothschild herself and the actress Jane Birkin – one-off designs that were not included in the couture house's runway show. The outfits for other clients, such as Nan Kempner, were taken from the Autumn–Winter 1971–72 haute couture collection. In accordance with the styles of the late 19th century, Yves Saint Laurent's dresses are characterized by sleek, flowing lines, counterbalanced by leg-of-mutton sleeves and high collars. The bows on the back of the gowns recall the swags of fabric typical of Proust's time, keeping the structure of the garments contemporary (without including a bustle) while accentuating the curve of the lower back. For the couturier, it was less about drawing inspiration from the past than offering a new take on the fashions – ephemeral by definition – of his times.

Displayed against the backdrop of one of the Musée d'Orsay's clock faces – a reminder of the original purpose of the building, first opened in 1900 and offering a spectacular view over some of the buildings of 19th-century Paris – Yves Saint Laurent's gowns seem to serve as a bridge between Proust's day and our own. A.A. & D.É.

1. Yves Saint Laurent, *L'Actualité*, 15 July 1991.

John Paxton, *View of the south and east facades of the Château de Ferrières*, 1853–56,
pencil, ink and watercolour on paper with retouching in white, Musée d'Orsay.
[Opposite] Yves Saint Laurent, gown design for Marie-Hélène
de Rothschild, Bal Proust, 1971, pencil on paper.
[Overleaf] Sketches for gowns for the Bal Proust, 1971, pencil on paper.

The Bal Proust was held at the Château de Ferrières on 2 December 1971. The château was built in the late 1850s for James de Rothschild by the architect Joseph Paxton. Paxton was world famous as the designer of London's Crystal Palace, built to house the Great Exhibition of 1851, the first in a series of major international exhibitions. The Musée d'Orsay owns three watercolour renderings of Paxton's original design for the Château de Ferrières, which was eventually rejected in favour of a different, more eclectic, design that borrowed from Italian and French Renaissance architecture.

Yves Saint Laurent received several commissions for outfits for the ball and produced a great many sketches of evening gowns with pinched-in waists and leg-of-mutton or ruffle sleeves in soft, flowing fabrics. Worn by slender women with their hair swept up into high chignons, these dresses were very reminiscent of the Belle Époque. Some of them had low necklines decorated with a fabric flower, like the one created for Madame Rochas. In pencil on paper, the sketches reflect the couturier's interest in movement, which can be seen in the gowns made for Jane Birkin and Marie-Hélène de Rothschild, flowing sashes and hat bands, billowing skirts and exaggerated shoulder lines creating a typically *fin de siècle* look.   A.A. & D.É.

192   Musée d'Orsay

Musée d'Orsay

Félix Nadar, *Portrait of Sarah Bernhardt*, 1859, salt print
from a collodion glass negative, Musée d'Orsay.
Cecil Beaton, *Baroness de Rothschild*, 1971, Cecil Beaton Archives.
[p. 196] *Hélène Rochas*, 1971, Cecil Beaton Archives.
[p. 197] *Marisa Berenson*, 1971, Cecil Beaton Archives.
[p. 198] *Jacqueline de Ribes*, 1971, Cecil Beaton Archives.
[p. 199] *Jane Birkin*, 1971, Cecil Beaton Archives.

Cecil Beaton was a photographer, illustrator and stage and film designer, a man who described himself as a 'fanatical aesthete'. Elegant and eccentric, a little obsessed with the past, he might have stepped out of the pages of Proust's novel. Beaton was a regular contributor to *Vogue* and was asked by the magazine to photograph the guests at the Bal Proust – rather in the manner of the great portrait photographer Félix Nadar. The guests were required to wear costumes inspired by characters from *À la recherche du temps perdu*. In designs by Yves Saint Laurent, Hélène Rochas dressed as Odette de Crécy, wearing white flowers around her décolletage, and Jane Birkin wore a Belle Époque gown, while Marisa Berenson became a spectacular version of the Marquise Casati, one of Proust's contemporaries. Each of the guests was both an actor and a spectator at the ball, transformed by Beaton's lens into a photographic fiction – something that would have delighted Proust himself, who regarded photography as a metaphor for 'involuntary memory'. He loved the medium and tried in vain to obtain a photograph of the Comtesse Greffulhe, the inspiration for his Duchesse de Guermantes. The countess – who reigned supreme over the Paris salons – was a friend of Paul Nadar, Félix's son and successor, and regularly posed at the Studio Nadar, which offered 'the image of eternal youth'.[1] Following the countess's example, the whole of artistic and bohemian Paris soon flocked to the studio, which became renowned for portrait work.   M.M.

1. Undated letter (probably from January 1920) from Marcel Proust to Élisabeth Greffulhe, cited in Sylvie Lecailler,
   La mode retrouvée, exh. cat., Paris: Musée Galliera, 7 November 2015–20 March 2016, Paris: Éditions Paris Musées.

Musée d'Orsay

198   Musée d'Orsay

Claude Monet, *Le Déjeuner sur l'herbe*, 1865–66, oil on canvas, Musée d'Orsay.
Yves Saint Laurent, 'Je vivrai un grand amour' bridal gown, Spring–Summer 1986,
white faille with black dot print.

Yves Saint Laurent held an ongoing dialogue with art, paying homage to various painters at different points in his career, not least among them Édouard Manet and Claude Monet. After he and Pierre Bergé bought the Château Gabriel in Benerville-sur-Mer in 1983 – formerly the property of Paul and later Gaston Gallimard, who published Marcel Proust's *À la recherche du temps perdu* – the couturier had the walls painted to resemble Monet's *Waterlilies.* As a connection in the other direction, Monet himself served as a model for the painter Elstir in Proust's novel. While the wedding dress in white faille with black polka dots – part of the Spring–Summer 1986 haute couture collection – inevitably conjures up images of Monet's paintings of women in pale crinoline gowns, the trouser suit (p. 205) more closely echoes Manet's *Le Déjeuner sur l'herbe*, a work that caused a scandal at the Salon des Refusés in 1863, thanks in part to the harsh contrast between the nude female figure and the men in their dark suits. From 1967 onwards, Yves Saint Laurent ensured that women too could benefit from the status and power associated with this most masculine of outfits. A.A.

Musée d'Orsay

[pp. 206–11] Yves Saint Laurent, sketches for costumes for the Queen and Édith de Berg in *The Two-Headed Eagle* by Jean Cocteau, 1978, felt-tip and pastel on paper.

In 1978, Yves Saint Laurent designed the sets and the costumes for a new adaptation of Jean Cocteau's *The Two-Headed Eagle*, directed by Jean-Pierre Dusséaux and produced by Pierre Bergé, who was then director of the Théâtre de l'Athénée in Paris. Fascinated by the stage and a great admirer of Cocteau, the couturier produced hundreds of sketches, which are now conserved at the Musée Yves Saint Laurent Paris.

Drawing his inspiration from late 19th-century fashions, he decided to deck the characters of the Queen and Édith de Berg in bustle gowns, long gloves, fans and elaborate hairstyles. In creating these voluminous outfits with all their flounces and frills, he was interested in establishing a relationship not merely between the accessories and the overall look but between clothing and movement. To that effect, he produced a series of sketches like rapid snapshots, a few lines sufficing to capture the flow of fabric or create an impression of energy, fluidity and movement not very far removed from the 'silent language of dresses' so dear to Proust. Proust himself was more focused on the relationship between garment and appearance than on garments themselves, and at the end of *Le Temps retrouvé* he wrote: 'I would construct my book, I dare not say ambitiously like a cathedral, but simply like a dress.'[1]

A.A. & D.É.

1. Marcel Proust, *Le Temps retrouvé* (1927), Paris: Gallimard, 'Bibliothèque de la Pléiade' coll., vol. IV, 1989, p. 610.

Yves Saint Laurent, sketches for headdresses and decorations for
the Bal des Têtes, 1957, gouache, pastels, ink and pencil on paper.

The Bal des Têtes was held at the Hôtel Lambert on 23 June 1957 by Baron Alexis de Redé, a key figure in café society, who noted in his memoirs that 'the guests were asked to come wearing specially made headdresses.'[1] He asked the young Yves Saint Laurent, then an assistant to Christian Dior, to design decorations and headdresses for the ball.

The drawings he made, mostly in gouache on coloured paper, revealed just how talented the young designer (then aged twenty-one) truly was. The delicate faces with their almond-shaped eyes and irregular features were inspired by the drawings of Christian Bérard, a French artist, illustrator and designer greatly admired by Yves Saint Laurent. The latter let his imagination run wild in these sketches, his enthusiasm palpable. Feathers, pyramids of flowers, ribbons, tulle, spangles abound, with one of the headpieces resembling a swan. The tables, meanwhile, were decorated with huge pineapple-shaped vases on wicker stands and candlesticks swathed in flowers, with matching torchères scattered throughout the hall.

The 'Bal des Têtes' echoes a passage in *Le Temps retrouvé,* the final volume of Marcel Proust's *À la recherche du temps perdu.* The narrator is at the home of the Princesse de Guermantes, where he encounters a great many people he used to know but has difficulty recognizing because 'each of them seemed to have made themselves up, generally with powder, which changed them completely'. Marked by the years, the bodies and faces of the characters in *À la recherche* are described by Proust in a now-famous gallery of descriptions, which may be likened to a philosophical reflection on the passage of time. A.A. & D.É.

1. Baron de Redé, *Souvenirs et portraits*, Paris: Lacurne, 2017.

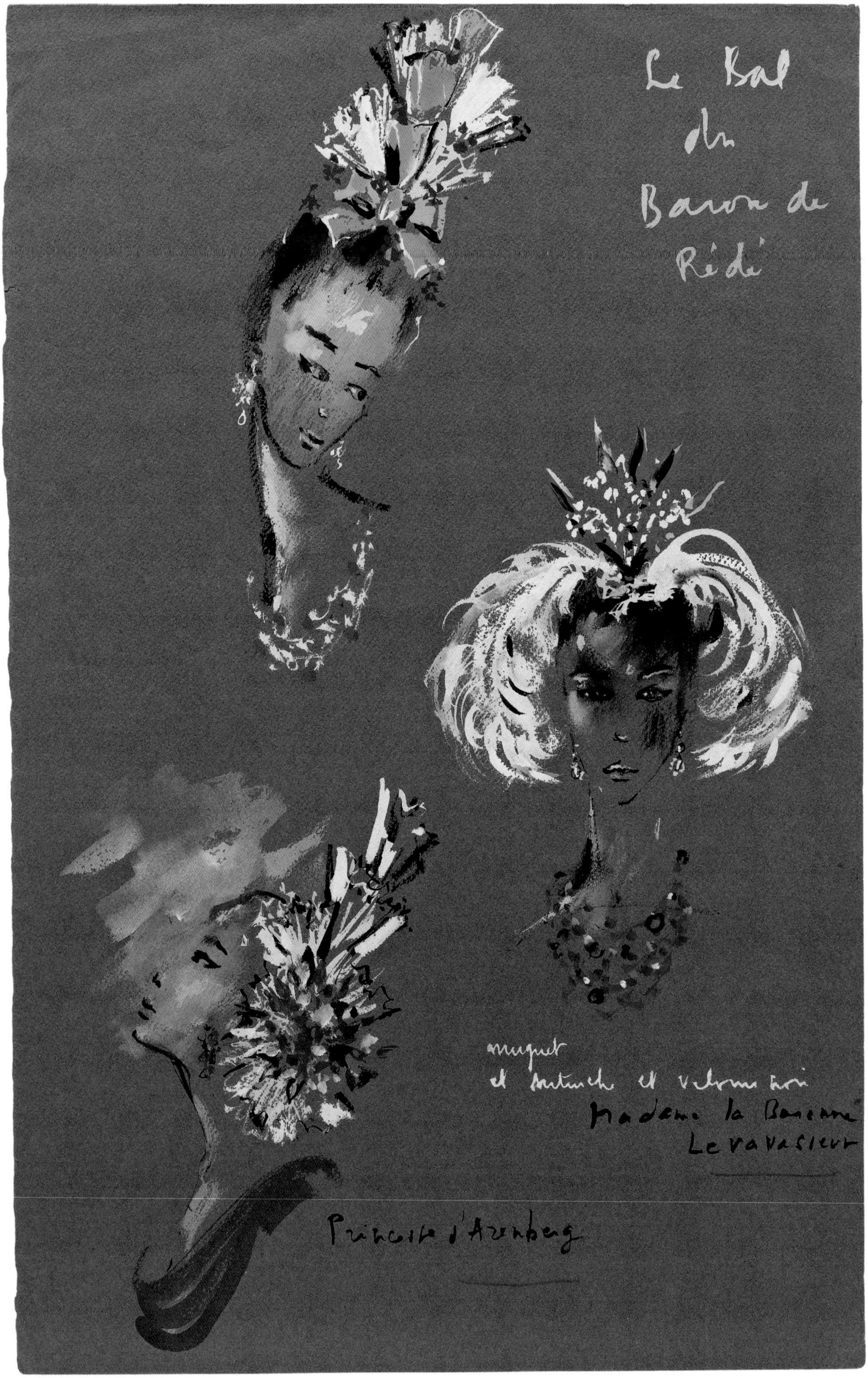

Le Bal
du
Baron de
Rédé

muguet
et autruche et vermenie
Madame la Baronne
Le Vavasseur

Princesse d'Arenberg

Le Bal du Baron de Ré'di

La Nuit   coiffure de tulle noir pailleté d'or.

Musée National Picasso, Paris

'Picasso is genius in its purest form.
His work is bursting with life and
honesty. Picasso is not purity.
Is he baroque? He has many careers,
many bows, and many strings
to each bow.'
Yves Saint Laurent

Yves Saint Laurent
and Pablo Picasso

Aurélie Samuel

[p. 216] Irving Penn, *Yves Saint Laurent*,
2 August 1983, Musée Yves Saint Laurent Paris.

In the foreword to the catalogue for the exhibition 'Dialogue avec l'Art', Dominique Païni drew a parallel between sewing and painting: 'Personal taste and visual acuity find in certain activities, such as painting and sewing, the same experimentation with line, the same precision in the handling of contrasts between materials and volumes.'[1] Yves Saint Laurent himself noted: 'What I love most is behaving as if I could sculpt light. Selecting a fabric, submitting to its lines, offering it up to the light, grasping its mystery... It's as if I were a painter, or a writer.'[2] One of the big differences between sewing and painting lies in the function of a piece of clothing, which obeys a commercial logic. Collections punctuate the process of creation, imposing limits on the couturier's freedom of expression. He is 'subjected to a contrary pressure, that is to say the mechanical recurrence of the "seasons", a commercial pressure disguised as a social ritual, which demands that he create according to a strict schedule, at regular intervals.'[3] The couturier is thus more constrained than a painter or sculptor working alone in a studio and creating art as inspiration strikes. Nevertheless, fashion, in the form of haute couture as opposed to ready-to-wear, demonstrated the couturier's creative genius and enabled him to free himself of commercial obligations.

Two artists, two collectors

Yves Saint Laurent and Pablo Picasso were two of the 20th century's most fascinatingly complex personalities. Both prolific artists, they created constantly, using multiple supports for their designs and approaching their work with absolute rigour. Their creativity was boundless and their approaches were similar when they were focusing on their respective media. 'The most important thing is the material, in other words the fabric and the colour,' Yves Saint Laurent declared. 'You can sketch a pretty design. You can put into a design all the knowledge you have acquired from your profession. But if you don't have the fabric, you lose your dress. [...] The anxiety is all about confronting the fabric and the colour, about having to handle the material – like the painter with his brushes, or the sculptor with his clay. And it's the material that has to be conquered if a dress is to match what you had in mind.'[4]

1. Yves Saint Laurent at the opening of his first retrospective show in France, Musée des Arts Décoratifs, Paris, May 1986.

2. Pablo Picasso, stage curtain designed for the ballet *Pulcinella*,
'Harlequin in the Ring with Ballerina and Rider', Paris, 1920, oil on paper, MNPP.

3. Yves Saint Laurent and Loulou de La Falaise at the
fittings for the Autumn–Winter 1979–80 collection.

Saint Laurent and Picasso both paid special attention to the places where
they worked. Their ateliers, like their homes, were places that reflected their
manner of working, their passions as embodied in the objects with which they
surrounded themselves, but also their personalities, in line with Émile Zola's
definition: 'A work of art is a corner of creation seen through a temperament.'[5]
These places of creation shared certain obvious similarities but also diverged
from one another in ways that photographs make clear: one is very orderly,
almost symmetrically so, while the other is apparently chaotic. Like Picasso,
who said 'The studio of a painter should be a laboratory. There, one does not
make art in the manner of an ape, one invents,'[6] Yves Saint Laurent allowed his
collections to mature in his studio, the heart of his couture house, in a hive-like
atmosphere. He arranged his favourite objects on his desk and pinned on his
cork display board any photographs and documents he thought would help his
creative process. Their homes were equally important to them both – Picasso's
Villa La Californie and Saint Laurent's houses in Tangier and Paris. The sur-
roundings were highly significant, but so were the interiors that reflected their
personalities and their creative visions via their choice of objects and how
they elected to position them. Picasso, as he himself said, defined a meaning-
ful space by arranging his own works inside his homes, in particular the Villa
La Californie. Sadly, however, no inventory of Picasso's belongings was made
at the time of his death, a fact greatly deplored by Laurent Le Bon.

Musée National Picasso, Paris

4. Yves Saint Laurent, evening ensemble worn by Vesna Laufer, Autumn–Winter 1979–80, photograph by Claus Ohm. 5. Day ensemble worn by Kirat Young, Autumn–Winter 1979–80. 6. 'Torero' evening ensemble worn by Mounia Orosemane, Autumn–Winter 1979–80.

Yves Saint Laurent and Pierre Bergé bought their first artwork – a Senufo bird – in 1960 and were passionate about collecting. Their focus on sub-Saharan art was part of a broader interest in African art, which the couturier explored in his Spring–Summer 1967 collection (see p. 44). Picasso also collected African art, which left a lasting mark on his work following his visit to the Musée d'Ethnographie du Trocadéro. Moreover, several artists in Saint Laurent and Bergé's collection could be found in Picasso's too: Cézanne, Modigliani, Chardin, Vuillard. In addition, Yves Saint Laurent continued a tradition not uncommon among couturier-collectors of acquiring works by Picasso himself: Paul Poiret bought the print *Circus Performers at Rest*, one Harlequin and several drawings by Picasso,[7] while Jacques Doucet acquired *Les Demoiselles d'Avignon* in 1924 via André Breton and was influenced by the painter for the rest of his life. Haute couture, from this point onwards, became saturated with fine art, absorbing its influences.[8] Bergé and Saint Laurent's zeal for collecting would also play its part in establishing the reputation of the work of Yves Saint Laurent, who 'while continuing the tradition of couturiers-collectors, was to be the first "couturier-artist".'[9]

Studying Picasso
Yves Saint Laurent and Pierre Bergé owned five works by Picasso, all dating from his Cubist period, between 1912 and 1917: *Man in an Armchair*, dating from the spring of 1912, exhibited in 1978 at the Grand Palais[10]; the drawing *Caricatures of Léonide Massine, Léon Bakst and Serge Diaghilev*, made in Rome in 1917, and which Yves Saint Laurent must have seen at the 'Diaghilev' exhibition in 1979[11]; *Man with Guitar* (1912–13); *Musical Instruments on a Table* (1914–15); and *Chicken, Glass, Knife, Bottle*, dating from the spring of 1913, acquired in 2002. Aside from the works that hung on his walls, Yves Saint Laurent knew Picasso from the many books he owned, among them Maurice Raynal's *Picasso* (1953), *Le Cubisme de Picasso* (1979) by Pierre Daix and Joan Rosselet,[12] and most notably *Picasso* (1955) by Frank Elga and Robert Maillard, all of them kept in the studio library at 5 avenue Marceau, or at his home, at 55 rue de Babylone. 'I start by working from home, sitting at a desk, which serves that purpose and no other,' the couturier said. 'The room consists of a mirror, a sofa and two bookcases. Those bookcases contain all the reserves I could wish to draw on. The works of Braque, Picasso, Juan Gris....'[13]

7. Yves Saint Laurent, 'Torero' suit worn by Dothi Dumonteil,
Autumn–Winter 1979–80, photograph by François-Marie Banier.

Like classical painters copying the old masters, Yves Saint Laurent copied Picasso, working from the reproductions in the Maillard and Elgar book. Some of the sketches he made are dated 1979, which suggests that the entire sketchbook – which is conserved in the Musée Yves Saint Laurent Paris – dates from that year.

These copies, executed in colour pencil and felt tip, reproduce whole paintings and, in some instances, just details of an original work – all material that fed into the couturier's own creations. It was a way of developing an in-depth knowledge of the painter's work. As Yves Saint Laurent himself said, 'My approach was not to measure myself against the greats, but to try to learn lessons from their genius.'[14]

The Autumn–Winter 1979–1980 collection

Few programmes for Maison Saint Laurent runway shows included a 'statement of intent' relating to the collection being shown. The one published for the Autumn–Winter 1979–80 haute couture show was therefore something of an exception. The collection was described from the outset as a 'homage to Serge Diaghilev and his collaboration with Picasso'. 'I had begun with matador suits, but my idea hadn't taken shape,' the couturier said. 'At the Bibliothèque Nationale, I saw an exhibition of the scale models of Diaghilev's sets for his ballets.[15] After Bakst's Eastern inspiration, there was a palpable sense of rupture caused by the war, and also a new upsurge, a flame, with *Le Tricorne* and *Parade*. My collection is based on that specific moment and constructed like a ballet. I used Picasso and a softer form of Cubism, the Harlequins, the Blue Period, the Rose Period, the *Tricorne* period, as my starting point. [...] Some collections, like this one, seem special to me and give me a feeling of artistic joy. [...] I worked with solid areas of colour, like a painter. There are a great many things about me that I express in this collection. I explore my interests, in terms of painting and literature. I let everything out through haute couture.'[16]

At the Bibliothèque Nationale exhibition, Yves Saint Laurent had admired Picasso's curtain designs for *Parade* – created in 1917 for the seventh season of the Ballets Russes at the Théâtre du Châtelet – and for *Pulcinella* in 1920 (fig. 2). The three major motifs of these works – bullfighter, ballerina and Harlequin – found their way into his 1979 collection (figs. 4, 5, 6). He later 'came across the costume designs that Picasso had made for Serge Diaghilev's *Le Tricorne*.'[17] 'The next day,' he said, 'I took a piece of black velvet and a blue velvet skirt and inserted velvet panels into the blue of the skirt. All the rest just

Musée National Picasso, Paris

happened, I remember it perfectly....'[18] The first design in the collection was, in fact, a blue and black suit in a mix of wool and velvet[19] (fig. 7). Saint Laurent's technique of using alternating colours to give a garment a geometric look harks back to Picasso's use of musical instruments as a motif, as demonstrated by the jacket worn by Paloma Picasso (fig. 9): a rough sketch for the jacket – in stiff fabric from the Bucol silk company – features a guitar (fig. 11) that recalls the artist's *Still Life with Guitar and Sheet Music* (fig. 10).

On the original sketch for dress no. 77, decorated with a woman's face,[20] there is a drawing of (among several other things) a guitar (fig. 12). With the help of Loulou de La Falaise,[21] Yves Saint Laurent would design a version of the jacket with the guitar in place of the face for the exhibition at the Musée des Arts de la Mode in Paris in 1986,[22] thus echoing Picasso's works in two and three dimensions.

Spring–Summer 1988 'Homage to Artists' collection

This 'Homage' collection comprised some 130 designs, of which thirty featured embroidery by the Maison Lesage, with whom Yves Saint Laurent had formed a close working relationship. These pieces represented painted surfaces in three dimensions by using a skilful combination of embroidery, sequins, ribbons and fabrics. Cubist motifs abounded. Asked one day why he had chosen to pay tribute to the painters he admired – Matisse, Mondrian, Van Gogh, Bonnard and Picasso, among them – Yves Saint Laurent responded: 'Because I have always felt a very close connection (albeit a modest one) between their art and my work. [...] I have tried to establish a real dialogue. [...] Without comparing myself in the least with those painters, it is true that my demands are similar.'[23] Once again, Yves Saint Laurent relied on sketches and copies that he had made, but also on the works by Picasso that he and Pierre Bergé had acquired, such as *Man with Guitar* (1912–13) – a gift, probably in the early 1980s, from Gustav Zumsteg, director of Maison Abraham and a personal friend of the couturier – and *Man in an Armchair*, executed in Céret in spring 1912 and purchased from Galerie Tarica in 1987, a work that combines collage and Indian ink on paper. Examination of the latter work was surely an influence on the couturier, most notably in the design of jacket no. 64.

The articles devoted to the collection in the press were highly complimentary, and *Vogue Paris* staged a photo shoot in which a model wearing the 'Cubist suit decorated with the body of a violin embroidered by Lesage',[24] posed inside in a Louis XVI-style frame, just like a painting.

The fabrics – some soft, some stiff – were handled in innovative ways. Some motifs – such as the birds inspired by Georges Braque[25] – were designed to extend beyond the natural line of the garment, like elements of a piece of sculpture. 'For three years, a book had lain on the low table in Yves Saint Laurent's living room: *Braque: the Complete Graphics* by Dora Vallier,'

8. Pablo Picasso, costume design for one of the four constables from the ballet *Le Tricorne*, 1919, gouache and Indian ink on pencil on wove paper, MNPP.

9. Yves Saint Laurent, jacket worn by Paloma Picasso,
Autumn–Winter 1979–80 haute couture collection, photograph by Horst P. Horst,
from a series published in *Vogue* (Paris), December 1979.

wrote Patrick Thévenon. 'And for three years, each time he entered the room,
the couturier felt "captured" by the cover illustration: a huge black bird hover-
ing above a square composition in four shades of green. But before he could
take the step – an inconsequential one for the mere reader – of picking up the
book and opening it, there had to be time for the work to mature. Because he
knew very well that for him, as an artist, that step would not lead to an hour or
two's diversion, but to several months' worth of exertion. [...] Once he opened
Dora Vallier's book, something dazzling occurred....'[26]

Although this collection references the work of Georges Braque
rather more than that of Pablo Picasso, Yves Saint Laurent drew considerable
inspiration from the Catalan artist's oeuvre for much of his career, and when,
in 1992, he was asked: 'Which painter do you feel a close affinity with at the
moment?', the couturier replied: 'Picasso, always.'[27]

1 Dominique Païni, foreword to the catalogue for the exhibition 'Yves Saint Laurent. Dialogue avec l'Art', Paris: Fondation Pierre Bergé –Yves Saint Laurent, 10 March–31 October 2004, p. 10.
2 Yves Saint Laurent, *L'Insensé*, 1991.
3 Patrick Mauriès, 'La mode: un art?', in *Encyclopædia Universalis*, Paris, 1989, p. 507.
4 Yves Saint Laurent, 'Portrait de l'artiste', interview with Yvonne Baby, *Le Monde*, 8 December 1983.
5 Émile Zola, *Mes haines: causeries littéraires et artistiques*, Paris: A. Faure, 1866.
6 Christine Poggi, *Cubism, Futurism, and the Invention of Collage*, New Haven, CT: Yale University Press, 1992, p. 268.
7 See Hélène Joyeux, 'Un certain 'esprit de collection': les collectionneurs français du monde de la mode (XXe-XXIe siècles)', doctoral thesis supervised by Philippe Dagen, defended on 19 September 2020, Université Paris I Panthéon Sorbonne, p. 103.
8 See Diana Vreeland, *Diana Vreeland*, New York: Ecco, reprinted 2012, p. 18.

9 Hélène Joyeux, *op. cit.*, p. 20.
10 See *Il y a 70 ans, 1908–1978: la grande aventure cubiste*, exh. cat., Paris: Grand Palais, March–April 1978, p. 45.
11 No. 216 in the catalogue *Diaghilev: les Ballets russes*, Paris: Bibliothèque Nationale de France, 17 May– 29 July 1979 (exhibition held to commemorate the 50th anniversary of Diaghilev's death).
12 This is the catalogue raisonné of works from the period 1907–16. The library contained other books on Picasso, including *Picasso. Pastelle, Zeichnungen, Aquarelle* (Werner Spies, 1986) and *Goodbye Picasso* (David Douglas Duncan, 1975).
13 'Saint Laurent: 30 ans de passion', *Elle*, January 1992.
14 *Yves Saint Laurent. Dialogue avec l'art*, 2004, *op. cit.*, p. 9.
15 See note 11.
16 *Vogue Paris*, September 1979, p. 272.
17 Colour reproductions of the original costume and set designs for *Le Tricorne*, no. 243 in the Bibliothèque Nationale catalogue.

10. Pablo Picasso, *Still Life with Guitar and Sheet Music*,
Paris, c. 1920, pochoir print with gouache on paper, MNPP.

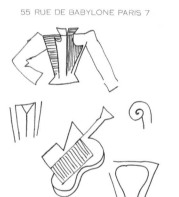

11 & 12. Yves Saint Laurent, original sketches, Autumn–Winter 1979–80,
felt-tip on paper, Musée Yves Saint Laurent Paris.

18 Yves Saint Laurent, *L'Actualité*, 15 July 1991.
19 'When I began to work with the idea – the first suit was turquoise wool and black velvet....', Bernadine Morris, interview with Yves Saint Laurent in *The New York Times*, 4 August 1979, p. 8.
20 See p. 238 in this book.
21 Almost certainly made by the costume designer Hector Pascual, the first conservator of the Yves Saint Laurent collection.
22 Yves Saint Laurent retrospective exhibition, Paris: Musée des Arts de la Mode (now the Musée des Arts Décoratifs), 30 May–26 October 1986.
23 'Yves Saint Laurent et l'Art', *Air France Madame*, August 1990.
24 'Yves Saint Laurent passionnément', *Vogue Paris*, 1 March 1988.
25 'The doves and the violins were inspired by Braque, [Yves Saint Laurent] said, not Picasso, as many viewers believed', in Bernadine Morris, 'Marriage of Fashion and Art by Saint Laurent', *The New York Times*, 28 January 1988.
26 'Le choc Saint Laurent – Dans le match de la mode, il sort une arme secrète: le Cubisme' by Patrick Thévenon, *Paris Match*, 12 February 1988.
27 'Saint Laurent: 30 ans de passion', *Elle*, January 1992.

Musée National Picasso, Paris

Works exhibited

Pablo Picasso, *Violin*, Paris, 1915, cut and folded sheet metal, paint and wire, MNPP.
Yves Saint Laurent, 'Homage to Pablo Picasso' jacket, Spring–Summer 1988,
black silk ottoman, embroidered with beads and sequins.
Yves Saint Laurent, Homage to Pablo Picasso' jacket, Spring–Summer 1988,
wool ottoman, embroidered with beads and sequins.

The Spring–Summer 1988 collection entitled 'Homage to Artists' took its inspiration from Cubism, and more specifically Georges Braque and Pablo Picasso. The aim was not to copy, but to 'set static things in motion on the body of a woman'. After drawing on Diaghilev's ballets for his 1979 collection, this time Yves Saint Laurent appears to have been looking at Picasso's collage work and his large-format compositions in oils focusing on the theme of musical instruments – as demonstrated by copies he made from the book by Frank Elgar and Robert Maillard. In fact, he was already interested in these themes as early as 1979, as we see from his studies for *Love* (1980), featuring guitars and violins.

Rather like Picasso's sculptures, the garment, this assemblage of fabrics, separate pieces of diverse elements, might be described as a juxtaposition of materials. Working on the toile, the first stage in the manufacture of a garment, is equivalent to the artist turning his initial sketch into a three-dimensional object. The *chef d'atelier* produces the toile as a test garment; it is fitted on a live model and then reworked so that the fabric hangs just right: 'There are three elements: the model, the material – the fabric, in other words – and the inspiration, me for example. It's this meeting between the three that enables the dress to take shape. [...] This is where the couturier finds himself in the position of a sculptor trying to shape his material.'[1]

1. Yves Saint Laurent, *Le Nouvel Observateur*, 1983.

Pablo Picasso, *Portrait of Nusch Éluard*, Paris, Autumn 1937, oil on canvas, MNPP.
Yves Saint Laurent, *Homage to Pablo Picasso* jacket, Autumn–Winter 1979–80,
blue, black and ivory wool.

This jacket from the Autumn–Winter 1979–80 collection is inspired by Pablo Picasso's *Portrait of Nusch Éluard*. Nusch was the 'face' of Surrealism, married to Paul Éluard in 1934 and muse to a number of artists including Man Ray, Dora Maar and Picasso. The latter painted several portraits of her from 1936 onwards. The one he painted in 1937 (housed in the Musée Picasso, Paris) shows her in an outfit designed by Elsa Schiaparelli, now lost, that was taken from the couturière's Autumn–Winter 1937–38 haute couture collection. The lapels were decorated with gilded cherubs by the jewelry designer Jean Schlumberger.[1]

Although Yves Saint Laurent was a great admirer of Schiaparelli – 'Madame Elsa Schiaparelli was incomparable. There is no equivalence to be found. Her imagination knew no bounds'[2] – the suit in his 1979–80 collection appears to be a reinterpretation of the garment as painted by Picasso rather than the original. The careful structuring of the fabric, using alternating bands of different colours to give a geometric look, continues the overall theme of the season,[3] and the glass earrings recall the Harlequins in that same collection. There is nevertheless a point of overlap between the two designers and their respective approaches: 'One gets a sense of a Mediterranean influence in Elsa Schiaparelli's work, as in that of Yves Saint Laurent, who exhibited the same thing, having spent his early years in Oran,' said Paloma Picasso.

It could well be supposed that Yves Saint Laurent admired Nusch Éluard and the way she chose to live, successfully establishing herself as a free spirit and a representative of the avant-garde. The couturier made his own contribution to the emancipation of women, inviting them to appropriate the male wardrobe and thereby assume the same responsibilities as men. Nusch Éluard was 'the most celebrated woman in the Surrealist movement, as muse, as model, and as artist'[4] and is a reminder of the subtlety of the relationship that exists between the artist and the model – one that Yves Saint Laurent explored throughout his career.   A.S.

1. Thanks to Marie-Sophie Carron de la Carrière, curator of the Musée des Arts Décoratifs, for providing this information.
2. Yves Saint Laurent, foreword, in Palmer White, *Elsa Schiaparelli: Empress of Paris Fashion*, New York: Rizzoli, 1986.
3. See pp. 220–27 in this book.
4. Chantal Vieuille, *Nusch. Portrait d'une muse du surréalisme*, Paris: Artelittera, 2010, p. 79.

Pablo Picasso, *Bust of a Woman in a Striped Hat*, Paris, 3 June 1939,
tempera on hardboard, MNPP.
Yves Saint Laurent, 'Homage to Pablo Picasso' dress, Autumn–Winter 1979–80,
black satin and velvet, embroidered with sequins and beads.

For each of his collections, Yves Saint Laurent made many sketches. While some of these were retained for the final selection, others – simple doodles or rough ideas relating to a particular motif – are today conserved in the archives under the heading 'concept sketches'. What they show us is that a garment designed by Saint Laurent is the product of a gradual process of synthesis. For the collection inspired by Picasso and Diaghilev, he filled whole pages of his notebook with copies of Picasso's works, based on reproductions published in *Picasso* (1955) by Frank Elgar and Robert Maillard. These efforts demonstrate the couturier's desire to acquire an in-depth knowledge of the great painter. One of the copies he made in this notebook is of the *Portrait of Marie-Thérèse Walter*, a drawing in coloured pencil which recalls – owing to the profile view of the face and the prominence of the eye – dress no. 77 in the collection. It is possible that Yves Saint Laurent saw this painting at the Picasso retrospective at the Grand Palais in 1979–80, marking the donation of many of Picasso's works to the French State in 1979.[1] In any event, we may concur with Bernard-Henri Lévy when he commented: 'Saint Laurent does not stick close, he quotes. He does not "quote"; he "interprets". He does not "interpret"; he mixes, mingles, blends, combines. And far from producing stupidly clever couture intent on trumpeting its references like so much noble ancestry, he produces genuinely intelligent couture that burns its references as soon as it has absorbed them.'[2]   A.S.

1. Exhibition entitled 'Picasso. Oeuvres reçues en paiement des droits de succession', Grand Palais, 11 October 1979–7 January 1980.

2. Bernard-Henri Lévy, foreword to *Yves Saint Laurent par Yves Saint Laurent*, reprinted in *Questions de principe II*, Paris: Le Livre de Poche, 1986.

'At the moment when the outlines
become clear and everything's
moving inside the house with
unbelievable speed and precision.
There's magic in the air,
we're all working together,
happy at the same time.'
Yves Saint Laurent

Saint Laurent
by Françoise Sagan

[p. 240] Andy Warhol, *Yves Saint Laurent*, 1979,
graphite on paper, Musée Yves Saint Laurent Paris.

Every year, a month before, people would start to say that it wasn't as good, that he was finished, that he was over, that his life and designs should be burned to the ground; every year, people believed he was dead to his friends and dead to the world of fashion, and every year, people would walk out of his first collection dazed and confused, and then, when they'd pulled themselves together, enchanted.

This tour de force, this complete change of heart within two hours, was a trick he was obliged to perform four times a year: twice a year for ready-to-wear, for which he was the first to lay down and maintain the standards – two collections a year – and twice a year for haute couture, which had brought him success and taken him to the very pinnacle of his art, allowing him to be playful and get his hands on the most extravagant, expensive and beautiful fabrics in the world. 'This is my luxury,' he said. He wouldn't have wanted to be without it. But if he had been forced to choose for once and for all between sumptuous and exorbitant haute couture and ready-to-wear, the odds are that Yves Saint Laurent, without hesitation, would have chosen ready-to-wear. First because he was a man of his time, and then because he never saw his couture designs in the street. He only ever came across them at evening events, galas and private dinners.

The rue Spontini was Yves Saint Laurent's past. It was there he reached his lowest point, twenty years earlier, when he had just left Dior and was starting out – with everything resting on his shoulders – in his own couture house: now, he was well aware, his first attempt had to be a masterstroke, or else it would be both his first and his last. Everyone came to see him bite off more than he could chew, and everyone came away dazzled. Since then, Saint Laurent has only had two flops. The first of these was in 1971 when he reworked the fashions of the 1940s, and all the women had shoulder bags, short skirts and platform soles. On that day, several wealthy women walked out at the start of the show: 'They didn't want, in their own words, to rub shoulders with tarts.' But there were other women, the inspired ones, the ones who could be called women of the world, the ones with a spirit of adventure, and a love of change that made them patrons of haute couture – albeit more thrifty patrons – who came and decided that it was sublime, and everyone else agreed. But Saint Laurent had been afraid.

He was afraid because any failure could potentially be fatal, and because four or five failures in a row would have meant a catastrophe, an end to creating haute couture with the enormous costs involved.

1. Yves Saint Laurent, Loulou de La Falaise and Anne-Marie Muñoz, in the studio at 5 avenue Marceau, Paris, 1982, photograph by Pierre Boulat.

2. Yves Saint Laurent and models Dominique Pommier, Anna Pawlowski, Elsa Faúndez de Dodero, Vesna Laufer, Jacqueline Miller and Nicole Dorier, in the salons at 5 avenue Marceau, Paris, 1974, photograph by Pierre Boulat.

Most of all, that would mean that he had stopped feeling that sense of intuition when he worked, that understanding of what women truly desire, here or elsewhere, the feeling that he felt every day in Paris and in his own head, and which always coincided so neatly with his own taste, the feeling that let him find inspiration in the exhausting but creative contemporary world, the constant sense of renewal, the theatrical splendour and constant surprises of everyday life.

From one year to the next, he knew, women could be – or could wish to be – young, mature, sad, restrained or tragic, just as they could wish to be joyful, witty or mysterious. If what they ultimately want to be is what Saint Laurent wants them to be, it's because they know that beneath the glitter and the novelty lies a vital, powerful and authoritative force, an intrinsic talent, a sense of taste, an imagination, a certainty, an elegance – in a nutshell, this fair-haired young man who never throws himself into extravagance and fantasy without the harmony and technique of his craft to guide him. Yves Saint Laurent presented his final collection, and he spoke about it with a smile of relief:

'Nothing was coming together, nothing looked like anything. It didn't matter how I draped my fabrics on the models' beautiful bodies: those gorgeous girls looked like nothing, nothing interesting at any rate. I was going crazy... I was making charmless, lukewarm Saint Laurent. I had a month and a half, as usual, to get everything done. And a month had gone by with nothing achieved. And then one day, quite by chance, I stood back and saw that I had *done* it: the dress had something to say, especially to the woman wearing it. I felt it straight away, and the model felt it too. It's hard to imagine how much of an unspoken connection exists between a couturier and a model. They [the models] sense when my imagination is engaged and they are gratified that their bodies – the way they move, the way they look – have sparked a creative response. They feel pleased and proud. I have a closer working relationship with these women than with anyone else. They are often exhausted but at times like this, they would do anything to help me.

It's a passionate profession: aside from me, who's [*sic*] no longer alive when things go badly, and never really happy with anything until the

3. Yves Saint Laurent during preparations for the Spring–Summer 1969 haute couture collection, in the studio at 30 bis rue Spontini, Paris, January 1969, photograph by Claude Azoulay. [pp. 246–247] Yves Saint Laurent and his models during preparations for the Spring–Summer 1969 haute couture collection, at 30 bis rue Spontini, Paris, January 1969, photograph by Claude Azoulay.

launch, there are also the seamstresses, the women who do the initial work by hand, and who are the holders and ultimate custodians of the secrets of haute couture (secrets passed on by their mothers, grandmothers, and so on.). Aside from these ladies – a dying race who will no longer have a purpose in our future society – there are the women who do the machine work, day and night, who are sometimes asked to start again from scratch, but to whom I would never do the disservice of making them perform work I didn't believe in myself; they would sense it and would despise me. The moment the creative work starts, the moment I feel I'm on my own, standing in the workshop issuing order after order, handing out job after job, not knowing whether this agitation, this frenzy that's been unleashed, will get me where I want it to, the moment everyone needs me, is looking at me, wanting to snatch the instructions, the ideas, straight from my lips, that's the moment when I feel responsible for everyone – all these teams of people, operating in every area of the firm. It's been tough, some years. I wouldn't find the theme, the idea, until ten days beforehand, and for ten days everyone would be going mad. And I would turn up, exhausted, in front of all these women who would be looking at me, some of them friends, and harsher *because* they were friends. During every months-long start to each of four collections, I no longer feel like myself at first. I feel like a prisoner. Empty. And then, one day, everything changes, and I'm the happiest of couturiers. I watch this guy moving around in front of me – working, finding ideas, inspiration – who is just another aspect of myself but whose achievements sometimes stagger me. Sadly, although I am one and the same person when things are going badly, there are always two of us when they are going well.

All my dresses are based on movement. A dress that does not reflect or make you think of a particular movement is not a good dress. Once you have discovered the motion in question – but not before – you can choose the colour, the final shape, the fabrics. The fact is that, in this job, you never stop learning.'[1]

1   Yves Saint Laurent, quoted in 'Saint Laurent par Françoise Sagan', *Elle*, March 1980, pp. 6–12

Musée Yves Saint Laurent Paris

Works exhibited

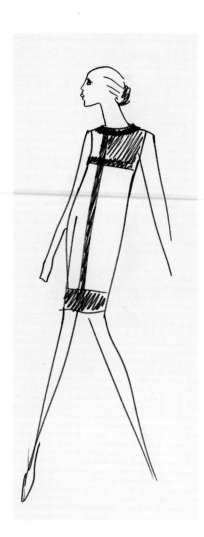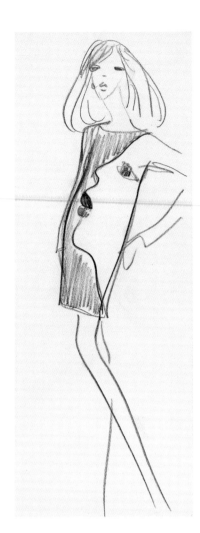

Yves Saint Laurent, original sketches chosen by the couturier for his farewell show at the Centre Pompidou on 20 January 2002, 1962–2002, graphite, felt-tip and pastel on paper.

We should say straightaway that fashion illustration is not something they teach at fine arts school, even though it is exactly the sort of 'daily prayer' that Delacroix thought essential for artists. Fashion illustration only came into being recently. By flouting the rules, it accesses all the more readily what is essential. A fashion illustration, like a photographic snapshot, freezes movement to a thousandth of a second, capturing gesture and crystallizing expression.

A successful fashion illustration is one that describes fabric and cut with utmost precision. Velvet and muslin are not drawn in the same way, any more than straight grain and bias cut, and if I say that Yves Saint Laurent has a unique, an incomparable, talent, if I assert this without fear of contradiction, it is because he has mastered all these things. An entire life is already present in a sketch of a dress.

For Yves Saint Laurent, a collection first has to be sketched; then comes the work on the body of the garment – fabrics suggested, tried, rejected, chosen. These are the *effets* [effects], so called. It's a marvel of the French language that the word should mean both impression and clothes. Finally, the dress goes off to the workshop – but not alone. It is accompanied by its sketch, which it must try to resemble. [...] The hand, we see, is fast, confident, precise. [The sketches] prove that Yves Saint Laurent is not just the great couturier we all know him to be: he is also stunningly good at producing fashion illustrations.

PIERRE BERGÉ[1]

1   'Yves Saint Laurent et le dessin de mode', first published in *Yves Saint Laurent par Yves Saint Laurent*, exhibition catalogue for 'Yves Saint Laurent: 28 années de création', Paris: Musée des Arts de la Mode, 30 May–26 October 1986, Paris: Herscher/Musée des Arts de la Mode, 1986, p. 33.

Pour Monsieur
Lesage
une
Veste d'après
le Bouquet
de Tourne
sols de
Van gogh

et
les
iris
de
Van gogh

J. Pierre 4034

"Catherine" 4079

jupe
porté
feuille
satin
marine

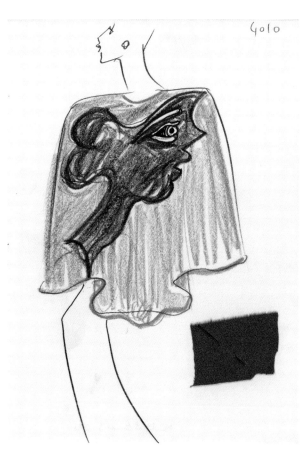

4010

Toile for a jacket made between 1980 and 2002,
cotton with pencil annotations and fabric swatch.
[Opposite, left] Atelier Madame Colette, toile for a gown with allover embroidery,
Spring-Summer 2001, white cotton gauze and black fabric appliqué.
[Opposite, right] Atelier Monsieur Jean-Pierre, toile for a tuxedo-style jumpsuit,
Autumn-Winter 2000-1, cotton and black ribbon.

Fashion moments are like musical moments: We know we're dealing with an instant poised in the present between the past and the future. The past is embodied in the sketch, the future in the finished garment. A dream takes form, arranged in white fabric, in what we call a toile [referred to as a 'muslin' or 'prototype' in English]. The toile is a bit like the couturier's parachute: It allows him to attempt this or that, to be inventive or daring without risk. He can start all over, as many times as necessary, until he achieves the desired result. A toile evokes emotion, as it represents an instant in time: a fashion moment. The toile will eventually be transformed into velvet, or satin, or other sumptuous fabrics. Embroideries are designed, sometimes cut from samples. The couturier places them on the toile and moves them around until they are exactly where they should be. Black bolduc ribbons are employed to indicate where the fabric should be cut or to delineate a shoulder or imply a curve. It is as if the couturier were a sculptor, endlessly kneading clay until it becomes a finished work, in this case the accomplished garment. The toile is the couturier's medium of choice. One could imagine a runway show of nothing but toiles, where the work of the couturier and the fashion house's ateliers could be displayed very matter-of-factly. We are sometimes disappointed with a fabric, but never with a toile. It is the toile that most faithfully transcribes the couturier's initial sketch. It is a chrysalis that, before our eyes, will become a butterfly.   PIERRE BERGÉ

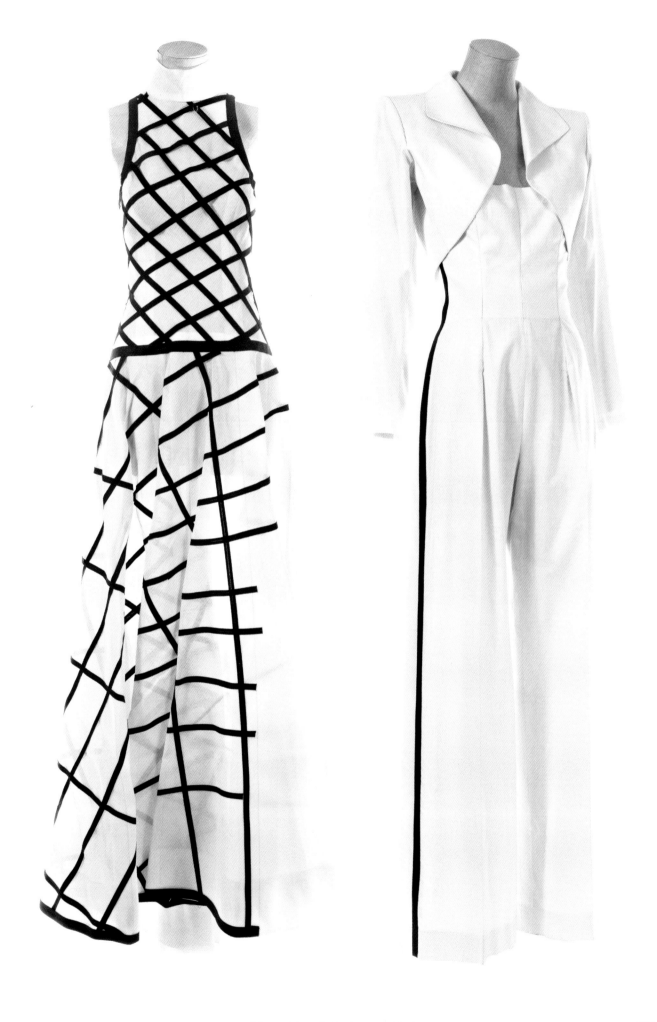

Musée Yves Saint Laurent Paris

[Opposite] Atelier Madame Jacqueline, toile for a 'Homage to Georges Braque' cape, Spring–Summer 1988, cotton and photocopy.
[p. 258] Atelier Madame Colette, toile for an ensemble inspired by Henri Matisse, Autumn–Winter 1999–2000, cotton and photocopy.
[p. 259] Atelier Madame Catherine, toile for a 'Homage to Georges Braque' gown, Spring–Summer 1988, cotton, cardboard and pastels.
[p. 260] Atelier Monsieur Jean-Pierre, toile for a 'Homage to Georges Braque' cape, Spring–Summer 1988, cotton and pastels.
[p. 261] Atelier Monsieur Jean-Pierre, toile for a 'Homage to Georges Braque' cape, Spring–Summer 1988, cotton and pastels.
[p. 262] Atelier Monsieur Alain, toile for a 'Homage to Georges Braque' cape, Spring–Summer 1988, cotton, graphite and black fabric appliqué.
[p. 263] Atelier Monsieur Jean-Pierre, toile for a 'Homage to Pablo Picasso' jacket, Spring–Summer 1988, cotton, black pencil and pastels.
[p. 265] Atelier Monsieur Yuksel, toile for a 'Homage to Pablo Picasso' jacket, Spring–Summer 1988, cotton, graphite and fabric appliqué.

258   Musée Yves Saint Laurent Paris

Musée Yves Saint Laurent Paris

Musée Yves Saint Laurent Paris

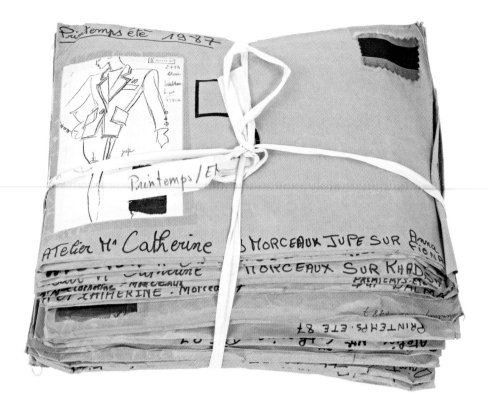

Envelopes filled with sewing patterns, marked with the name of the
premier d'atelier, the season, the collection and the design number.
[p. 268] Atelier Monsieur Jean-Marie, pattern for a blouse, 3 of 4 pieces,
Autumn–Winter 1990–91, cotton and felt-tip.
[p. 269 above] Atelier Monsieur Jean-Marie, pattern for a jacket, 3 of 9 pieces,
Autumn–Winter 1990–91, cotton and felt-tip.
[p. 269 below left] Atelier Monsieur Jean-Marie, pattern for a jacket, 4 of 11 pieces,
Autumn–Winter 1990–91, cotton and felt-tip.
[p. 269 below right] Atelier Monsieur Jean-Marie, pattern for a pea coat, 1 of 7 pieces,
Spring–Summer 1990, cotton and felt-tip.

Everything begins with the dreams of Yves Saint Laurent.

In these dreams, there are fantasies, longings and wishes, soon to be turned into magnificent designs. Sketches were always the starting point for Yves Saint Laurent's four annual collections, two haute couture and two ready-to-wear. First he worked on them in his Paris apartment on the rue de Babylone or in his Marrakech hideaway, and later at the Château Gabriel in Normandy. He knew that his ateliers could bring his precise lines to life and that Anne-Marie Muñoz, the studio director, would assign each design to the *premier d'atelier* who could best do it justice. Each *premier d'atelier* had their own particular talent or speciality.

The *premiers d'atelier* play a key role in a couture house. It is their job to study each sketch and grasp the dynamic of each design before work begins on the toile, a prototype garment. The toile is to the finished piece what a plaster cast is to a sculpture. It's usually made from unbleached calico but can vary in weight according to the fabrics that will be used for the finished design; gauze may be used in place of chiffon or tulle. This detail is usually noted on the sketch by Monsieur Saint Laurent; in the absence of other instructions, it's the impeccable eye of Madame Muñoz who interprets the couturier's intentions.

All notes are written directly on the toile in pencil, and the positions of decorative elements are marked, along with any other information needed to create the garment, starting with the direction of the fabric, straight grain or bias. All the secrets of couture are right there in the toile. When the *chef d'atelier* deems that the toile is ready, it is shown to Madame Ida, the technical director, who in turn decides whether it can be presented to Monsieur Saint Laurent. This process takes place in a small room adjacent to the studio. In intimidating silence, the models of the *cabine* – who

Musée Yves Saint Laurent Paris

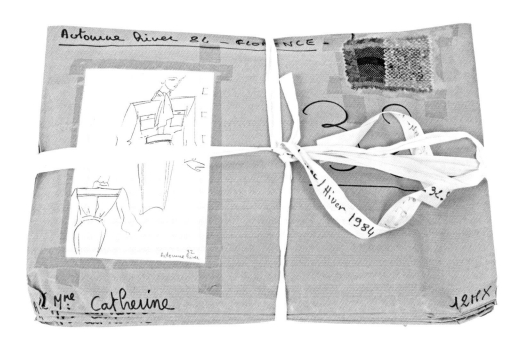

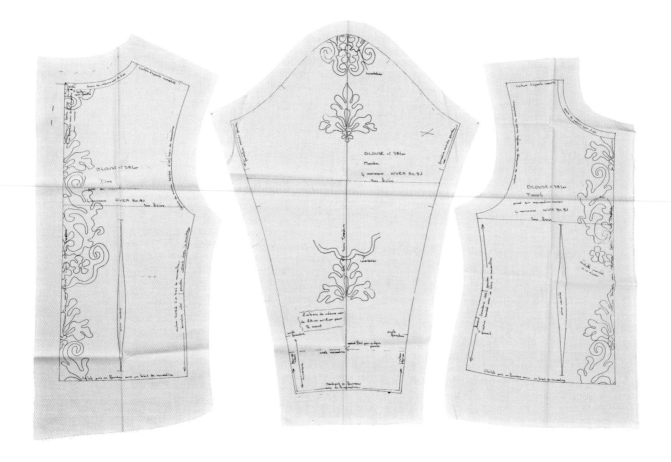

work full time for the house – put on the toiles, which are fitted by the *premier d'atelier*. Then they walk one by one, in ritual fashion, into the studio, where the couturier and his entourage are waiting expectantly. It's a moment of great tension, and everyone anxiously awaits Monsieur Saint Laurent's reaction. He alone can give the seal of approval. If he smiles, everyone smiles; if he frowns, everyone wishes they were somewhere else. Fortunately, smiles are much more frequent, owing to the talent of his teams who do their utmost to achieve the desired results for every collection. The traditional mirror ceremony now begins. Once the first impression has been made, the future of the design lies in its reflection in the mirror. The model walks as she would on the runway, striking poses that will make the toile look its best. The master's eye sees everything. He shortens the jacket by a centimetre, lengthens a sleeve, adds a pocket, removes a collar, adjusts the fall of a sash belt, alters the angle of a lapel. His sense of proportion is innate.

Once he is satisfied, it's time to pinpoint the fabric that should be used for the design, right down to the precise choice of lining. Monsieur Saint Laurent has a very clear idea of what he wants, but Madame Muñoz and Loulou de La Falaise also get a say in the final selection. The process is the same for every piece in the collection, from the simplest top to the most magical evening gown. When a toile passes the test, the *premier* rushes to announce the good news to the atelier. From then on, there is no room for error. They must cut, construct, stitch, press and finish, with not a second to lose. A collection is generally created within a very short period, a month at most, which is hardly any time at all, given the perfect finish that each piece requires. Nor must anyone forget the needs of the embroidery ateliers, whose work plays a key role in the house's reputation. One more stage is required before the final presentation: a rehearsal of each stage in the runway show. The couture house becomes a hive of activity, with everyone working day and night to capture the couturier's vision. It's time for final adjustments, full accessories, a finished vision. And then the moment to unveil the new collection arrives.

It's Wednesday, it's 11 a.m. and Pierre Bergé, who has been keeping a watchful eye on every detail since the very start, announces that the show is ready to begin. S.J.

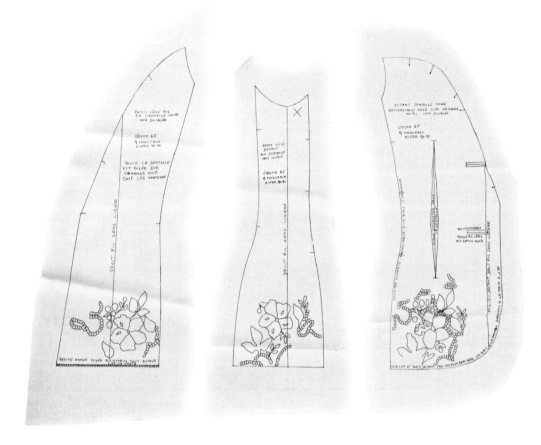

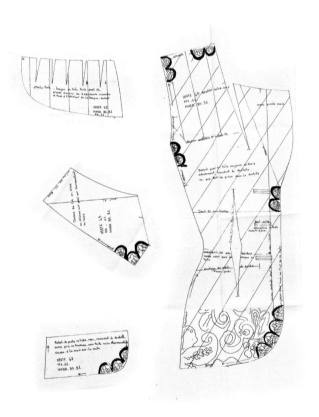

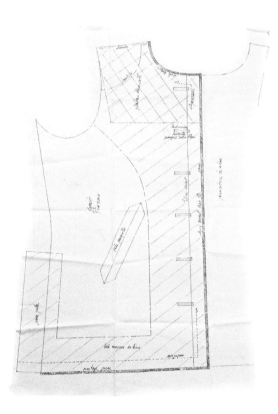

AH85
66 Lorelei 2339

Polaroid taken by couture house staff, Autumn–Winter 1985–86.
[p. 271] Shoe forms, wood and graphite.
[pp. 272–73] Shoe patterns, paper, felt-tip, pencil and paper clips.
[pp. 276–77] Hat forms and hat blocks, 1962–2002, plant fibre, wood and graphite.

Yves Saint Laurent did not like fashion. That may sound hard to believe of a designer who, for decades, exerted such an influence on fashion. What he did love was being a designer. He loved clothes, the power of clothes; and he loved accessories, every element, from head to toe, that serves to finish off an outfit. Fashions come and go, but Yves Saint Laurent constructed a style. From the moment he founded his own couture house, in 1962, he was laying the foundations of what would become the Saint Laurent look.

It was a time when women wore hats, and Yves Saint Laurent designed hats that were effortlessly beautiful. Fashion moved on, but his love of headwear endured and in the years that followed, he continued to design these crowning adornments for his clients. Not a single type of headgear escaped his attention, from boaters to wide-brimmed hats, berets to cloches, hoods to caps, turbans to scarves, fedoras to fur hats, and even including crowns of flowers, ears of corn or coloured stones. No one else delighted quite like Yves Saint Laurent in a display of feathers or a dazzling bandeau around the forehead, a Chinese cone hat or a Cubist composition. The couturier was clearly enjoying himself. And it worked: the results were delightful.

Yves Saint Laurent devoted equal attention to shoes. And here too he drew on – and adapted – classical styles. His favourites were court shoes, closely followed by strappy, high-heeled sandals (the 'Raymonde' – to give just one example – was the signature shoe from his 1971 'Liberation' collection), along with brogues, T-bar sandals and Mary Janes, with the occasional pair of heeled loafers, along with espadrilles and, occasionally for summer, Roman sandals, and of course those other favourites of his – boots of all types, high boots, ankle boots and more. His first shoe shop in rue du Faubourg-Saint-Honoré was wittily named 'La Bottique'.   S.J.[1]

1 The author would like to thank Cristelle Posada, apprentice and then *première de l'atelier* from 1984 to 2002, and Françoise Picoli, designer then collection director from 1977 to 2000, for their valuable help.

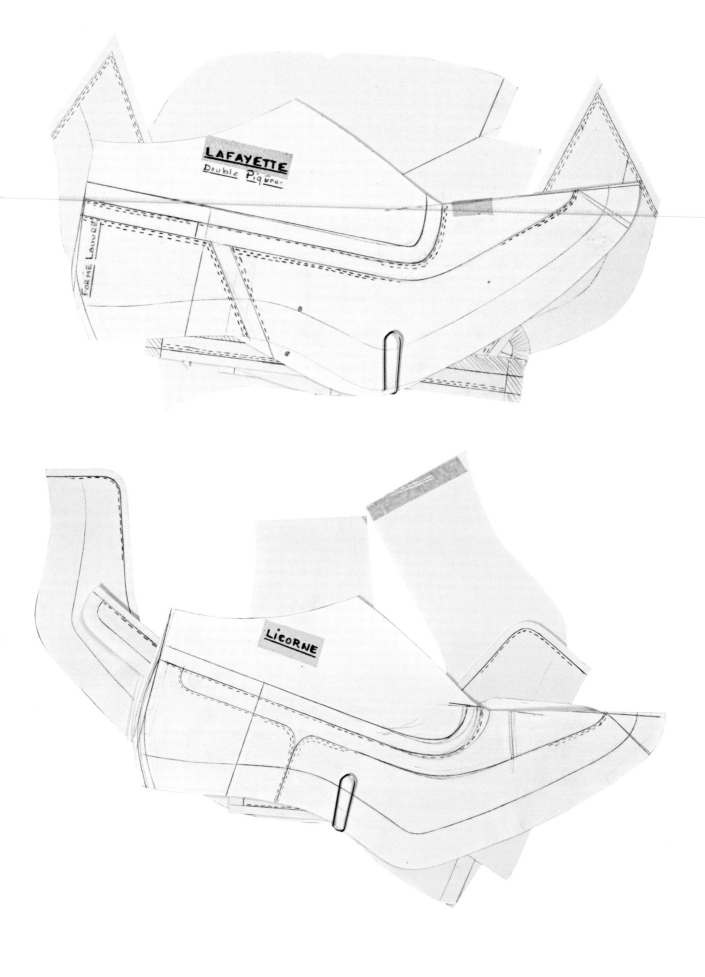

Musée Yves Saint Laurent Paris

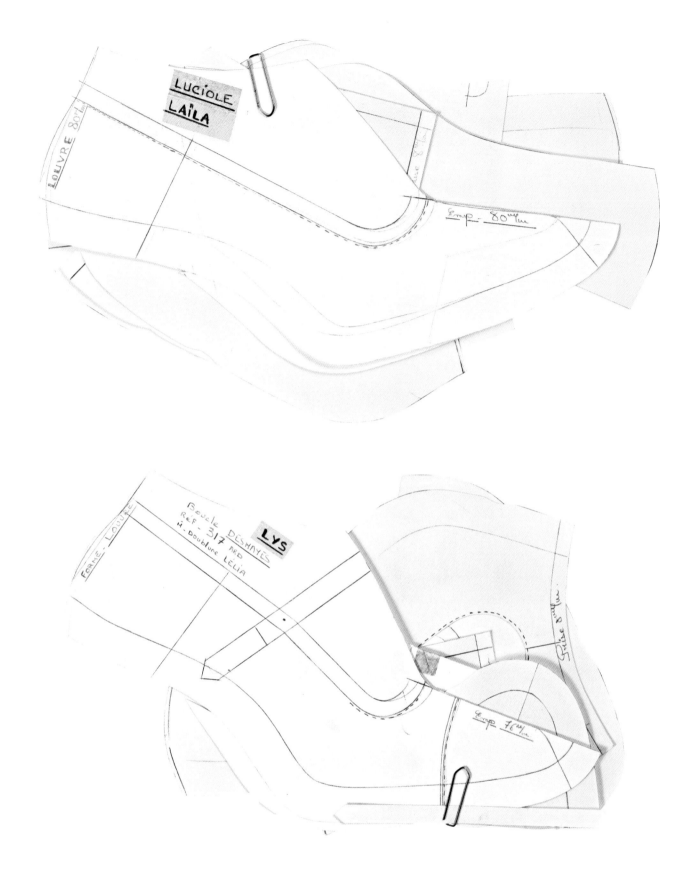

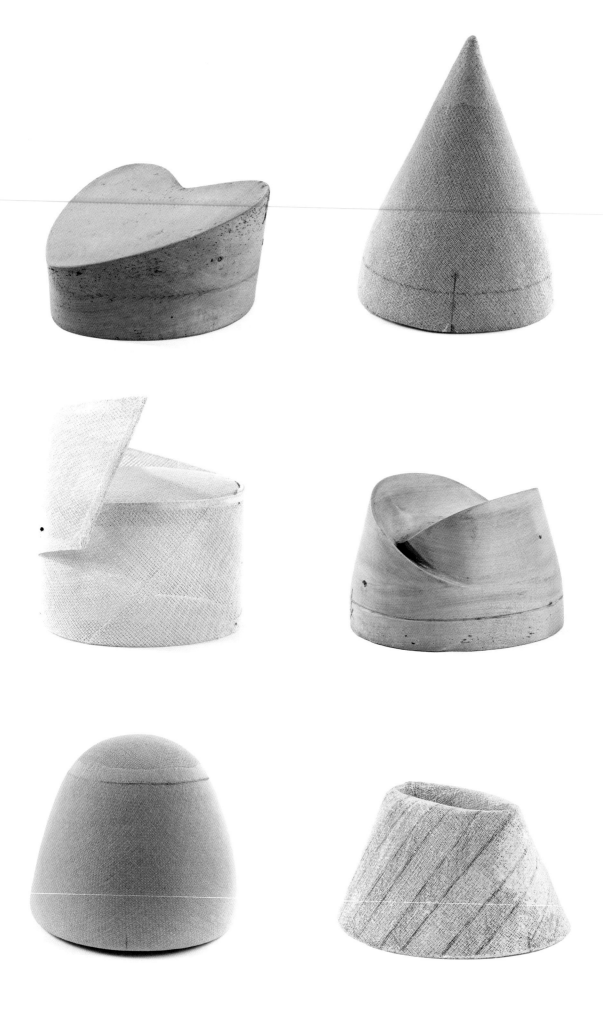

Musée Yves Saint Laurent Paris

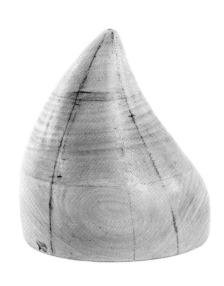

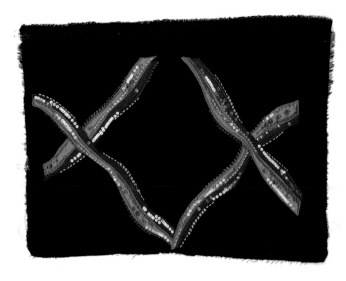

Embroidery and appliqué swatches commissioned by Yves Saint Laurent,
made by Lanel, Lesage, Montex and other French embroidery workshops, 1962–2002.

Throughout his career, Yves Saint Laurent combined purity of line with a love of exuberant ornamentation. From his earliest collections, the couturier made the utmost use of the talents of Paris's many haute couture craft ateliers. The arrival in 1972 of Loulou de La Falaise – friend, partner and collaborator – as head of accessories resulted in an outburst of creative energy. Embroidery swatches, scarf designs and buttons give a glimpse into this passionate interest, which was shared with the finest specialist artisans, all of whom utilized the skill of their workshops to meet the demands of the couturier's boundless imagination.

Yves Saint Laurent elevated the craft of embroidery far beyond its time-honoured decorative function. With his signature motifs – hearts, clover leaves, bows, ears of wheat – and opulent themed collections, or his homages to artists or to the arts of Africa, all of his creations bear witness to his love of this artform. Some of his embroidered pieces are almost jewels in themselves.

M.M.

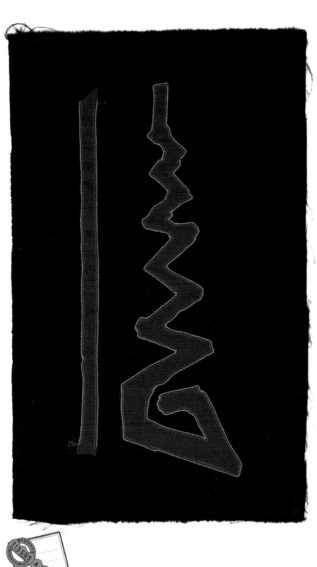

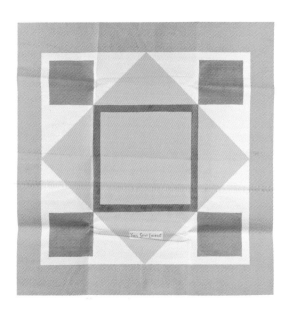

Original prints for Yves Saint Laurent scarves, made by the Maison Abraham,
1970s, screenprint on blotting paper.

Alongside other forms of ornament, Yves Saint Laurent used his great artistic intelli-
gence to design striking scarves, featuring unique combinations of colours, lines and
motifs. The prints shown here allow us to admire the formal beauty of the couturier's scarf
designs. In fact, they are working prints on blotting paper, created by the fabric ateliers
– in this case, the Maison Abraham – based on instructions and colour palettes provided
by the Yves Saint Laurent studio. These working documents allowed the couturier to
choose the most attractive colour schemes before the fabrics were printed. These prints
now bear witness to the huge repertoire of shapes and colours that the couturier used, in
an apparently inexhaustible range of combinations and variations.

M.M.

Musée Yves Saint Laurent Paris

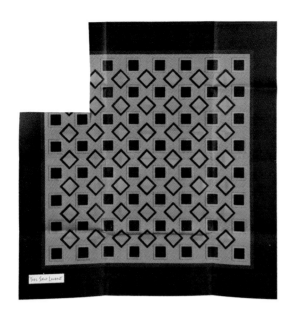

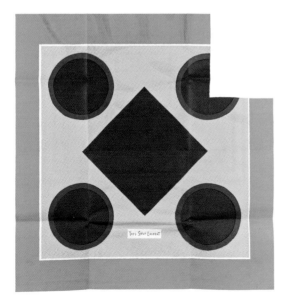
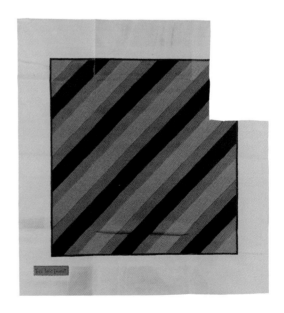

Naomi Campbell wearing the 'Homage to Vincent Van Gogh' jacket,
Polaroid taken by couture house staff, Spring–Summer 1988.
Yves Saint Laurent, 'Homage to Vincent Van Gogh' jacket, Spring–Summer 1988,
embroidered with sequins, beads and ribbon by the Maison Lesage.

Before a collection show, Polaroids are taken as a record of the accessories selected for each outfit. They were first used in 1969, but became standard from 1980 onwards, until the closing of the house in 2002. The instant nature of the Polaroid, its direct relationship with reality and the present moment, as well as its ease of use, all appealed to Yves Saint Laurent. The images record a happy and lively working atmosphere. They also provide a glimpse into the intimate world of the house, revealing particular aspects of the couturier's way of seeing and doing things. Sometimes the garments in these image appear to be unfinished, like the 'Homage to Vincent Van Gogh' jacket, inspired by the various versions of *Sunflowers* that the artist painted in 1888 and 1889.

Here the jacket is captured in an incomplete state, while the making process is still ongoing. Once finished, the jacket, covered all over in embroidered sunflowers, resembled an endless space in perpetual motion. Somewhere between a garment and a work of art, an ornament and a feat of skill, Yves Saint Laurent managed to make the jacket itself vanish, leaving only the painted motif, recreated by master embroiderer François Lesage, whose prodigious talents brought the couturier's ideas to life.

This jacket became one of the most sensational and newsworthy garments in fashion history and a major milestone in the appreciation of the work of Van Gogh in the 20th century. A wearable work of art, it is also one of the symbols of this magnificent exhibition. M.M.

Conclusion

Yves Saint Laurent remains one of the most important fashion designers of the second half of the 20th century. He is not the only one, far from it. Cristóbal Balenciaga and Gabrielle Chanel also made their mark, but Yves Saint Laurent had the dynamism of youth on his side, during a time of great social change.

His appointment as the successor to Christian Dior at the age of twenty-one brought him to the world's attention, and the success of his first collection earned him the nickname 'the little prince of fashion'. When he founded his own couture house, he soon became 'the king of fashion', a title justified by the global influence of his work. And a king he remained, even during the toughest times in his career.

From his childhood in Algeria onwards, he was enchanted by all forms of art, which he discovered through the pages of French magazines. This passion expanded to embrace theatre, cinema, music, literature and dance, as well as painting and sculpture. Through the gaze of this rapt young man, his creations began to be born.

Although Yves Saint Laurent was proud to be an artisan, his perceptiveness and his understanding of art nonetheless made him an artist. He always acknowledged the importance of the works that inspired him: those of Matisse and Picasso, of course, but also the works of many other great masters throughout his collections. 'Goya pink' and 'Frans Hals black', a bride inspired by Vélasquez's *Las Meninas*, Manet's bullfighters, Proust's ambiguous figures, Bonnard's gardens, Botticelli's *Birth of Venus*, Christian Bérard: all of his favourites were revisited in his collections, along with his contemporaries – Pop art, Cocteau, Visconti, Wesselmann, followed by his friends, from Sagan to Warhol, and of course the *coup de théâtre* that was Mondrian in the Autumn–Winter 1965–66 collection.

The fact that five of the most prestigious museums in Paris have chosen to host the work of Yves Saint Laurent, in collaboration with the Musée Yves Saint Laurent, is not only a way to celebrate the 60th anniversary of the founding of his couture house but also a means of granting him his rightful place as an artist, whose work engages in a dialogue with his peers in a way that few others can emulate.

The couture garments featured in this exhibition are displayed without accessories. This choice is in no way meant to deny the wider talents of the couturier who spent forty years adorning women with the most beautiful of ornaments. It was simply dictated by the greatest respect for his craft, in which everything is calculated to the millimetre, and in which the precision of cut, the balance of proportions and the quality of finish are paramount. These wonderful works are the products of a hive of workers, in which all the members of the house and its suppliers play a part, like worker bees feeding their queen. They give an insight into the hard work that took place in the building at 5 avenue Marceau, which is now the Musée Yves Saint Laurent Paris.

While the extensive archives conserved by the Fondation Pierre Bergé–Yves Saint Laurent will surely be the subject of further wonderful shows in future, this particular exhibition will undoubtedly be a landmark in fashion history, just like the Yves Saint Laurent retrospective organized by Diana Vreeland in 1983 at the Costume Institute of Metropolitan Museum of Art, New York.

STEPHAN JANSON

Chronology

1 August 1936

Birth of Yves Mathieu-Saint-Laurent in Oran, Algeria

1946

He sees Molière's *L'École des femmes*, in Oran, directed by Louis Jouvet, with sets by Christian Bérard

1951

Yves Mathieu-Saint-Laurent copies and illustrates various books, including Gustave Flaubert's *Madame Bovary*

1954

He discovers Marcel Proust's *À la recherche du temps perdu*

1954

Arrives in Paris

June 1955

He is introduced to Christian Dior, who immediately hires him as an assistant

1956

He designs decorations and headdresses for the Bal des Têtes, held by the Baron de Redé at the Hôtel Lambert

October 1957

Death of Christian Dior

November 1957

Appointed artistic director of Maison Dior, at the age of 21

1958

Meets Pierre Bergé

July 1960

Final collection for Maison Dior

1960

He and Pierre Bergé acquire a Senufo bird sculpture – the start of their art collection

July 1961

First offices for the future couture house are set up at 66 rue La-Boétie, 8th *arr.*, Paris

4 December 1961

Official opening of the Yves Saint
Laurent couture house
Cassandre designs the YSL logo.

29 January 1962

The first collection is shown at the
house's new premises at 30 bis rue
Spontini, 16th *arr.*, Paris

1963

Anne-Marie Muñoz joins the
house as studio director, a post
she holds until 2002

1965

'Homage to Piet Mondrian' dresses
(Autumn–Winter)

1966

Launch of the ready-to-wear line
Saint Laurent Rive Gauche; the
first shop opens at 21 rue
de Tournon, 6th *arr.*, Paris

1966

'Homage to Pop Art' collection and
first tuxedo (Autumn–Winter)

1966

Visits Marrakech with
Pierre Bergé and buys the
Villa Dar el-Hanch

1967

Collection inspired by African art
(Spring–Summer)

1968

Meets Andy Warhol

1969

Collaborates with the sculptor
Claude Lalanne (Autumn–Winter)

1971

'Liberation'/'Scandal' collection
(Spring–Summer)
Designs gowns for the
Bal Proust in December

1972

Loulou de La Falaise comes
to work at the studio

1972

Andy Warhol creates a series
of portraits of him

1974

The house moves to 5 avenue
Marceau, 16th *arr.*, Paris

1974

Buys the Villa Dar es Saada
in Marrakech

1976

'Opera – Ballets Russes' collection
(Autumn–Winter)

1977

'The Spaniards and the Romantics'
collection (Spring–Summer)
'Chinese' collection
(Autumn–Winter)

1979

'Homage to Picasso' collection,
(Autumn–Winter)

1980

'Shakespeare and the Poets'
collection, including homages to
Louis Aragon, Guillaume
Apollinaire and Jean Cocteau
(Autumn–Winter)

1980

Buys the Jardin Majorelle and
Villa Oasis in Marrakech

1981

Collection inspired by Henri
Matisse and Fernand Léger

1983

Exhibition at the Costume
Institute at New York's
Metropolitan Museum of Art

1983

Buys the Château Gabriel,
in Benerville-sur-Mer

1985

Exhibition at the National Art
Museum of China, Beijing

1986

Exhibition at the Musée des Arts
de la Mode, Paris
Exhibition at the Tretyakov
Gallery, Moscow

1987

Exhibition at the State Hermitage
Museum, Saint Petersburg
Exhibition at the Art Gallery of
New South Wales, Sydney

1988

Runway show at the Fête de
L'Humanité, La Courneuve

1988

'Cubist' collection
(Spring–Summer) and 'Homage
to Vincent Van Gogh'

History of the couture house	Collections and creations	Biographical details
1990 Retrospective at the Sezon Museum of Modern Art, Karuizawa	**1990** 'Homages' collection (with homages to Marcel Proust, Bernard Buffet, Marilyn Monroe, Catherine Deneuve, Christian Dior, Françoise Sagan, Christian Bérard, Maria Callas, Zizi Jeanmaire and more) (Spring–Summer)	**1990** Buys the Villa Mabrouka in Tangier
	1992 Collection inspired by Henri Matisse in Morocco (Spring–Summer)	
1993 'Yves Saint Laurent: Exotismes' exhibition at the Musée de la Mode, Marseilles		
	1995 'The Infantas' collection (Autumn–Winter)	
	1997 Collection inspired by the Court of the Valois and François Clouet (Autumn–Winter)	
1998 Runway show featuring 300 designs at the Stade de France, Paris, during the World Cup final		
	1999 Collection featuring a version of *The Romanian Blouse* (Autumn–Winter)	
	2001 Collection with dresses inspired by Pierre Bonnard (Spring–Summer)	
2002 Retrospective show at the Centre Pompidou, Paris Closure of the couture house Creation of the Fondation Pierre Bergé–Yves Saint Laurent	**2002** Final collection (Spring–Summer)	**January 2002** Yves Saint Laurent bids farewell to haute couture
2004 The Fondation Pierre Bergé–Yves Saint Laurent stages its first exhibition, 'Yves Saint Laurent: Dialogue avec l'art', on the former site of the couture house		

2008

The exhibition 'Yves Saint Laurent:
Diálogo con el arte' is held at
the Caixa Galicia Foundation,
La Coruña, Galicia

June 2008

Death of Yves Saint Laurent

2008–2009

Touring retrospective at the
Montreal Museum of Fine Arts,
then at the de Young Museum,
San Francisco

2009

'Yves Saint Laurent: Extraordinary
Journeys' exhibition at the Centro
Cultural Banco do Brasil,
Rio de Janeiro

2009

Yves Saint Laurent and Pierre
Bergé's art collection is sold

2010

Retrospective at the
Petit Palais, Paris

2011

Exhibition at the Fundación
MAPFRE, Madrid

2012

Exhibition at Denver Art Museum

2015

'Yves Saint Laurent: Style is
Eternal' exhibition at Bowes
Museum, Barnard Castle

2016–2017

'Yves Saint Laurent: The Perfection
of Style' touring exhibition at
Seattle Art Museum, then at the
Virginia Museum of Fine Arts

2017

Opening of the Musée Yves Saint
Laurent Paris and the Musée Yves
Saint Laurent Marrakech

8 September 2017

Death of Pierre Bergé

2017–2021

The two museums hold exhibitions
including 'L'Asie rêvée' (Paris,
October 2018–January 2019) and
'Une amitié marocaine: Tamy Tazi,
Fernando Sánchez et Yves Saint
Laurent' (Marrakech,
October 2021– May 2022)

List of works exhibited

[p. 22]
Jeanloup Sieff
Yves Saint Laurent
1971
Silver gelatin print,
30.5 × 30.1 cm
Paris, Centre Pompidou,
Musée National d'Art
Moderne – Centre
de Création Industrielle,
acquired by the State 1983,
attribution 1988
AM 1988-834

[p. 38]
Pablo Picasso
The Violin
[1914]
Oil on canvas, 81 × 75 cm
Paris, Centre Pompidou,
Musée National d'Art
Moderne – Centre
de Création Industrielle,
gift of Raoul La Roche, 1953
AM 3165 P

[p. 39]
Yves Saint Laurent
'Homage to Georges
Braque' cape
Spring–Summer 1988
Wool embroidered with
sequins, beads and buckskin.
Musée Yves Saint Laurent
– Paris
HC1988E128

[p. 42]
Pablo Picasso
*Harlequin and Woman
with Necklace*
Rome, 1917
Oil on canvas, 200 × 200 cm
Paris, Centre Pompidou,
Musée National d'Art
Moderne – Centre
de Création Industrielle,
legacy of Baroness Eva
Gourgaud, 1965
AM 3760 P

[p. 43]
Yves Saint Laurent
'Homage to Pablo
Picasso' gown
Autumn–Winter 1979–80
Black and white satin crepe
Musée Yves Saint Laurent
– Paris
HC1979H101

[p. 44]
Reconstruction of a wall
in André Breton's studio,
42 rue Fontaine, 1922–66
Paris, Centre Pompidou,
Musée National d'Art
Moderne – Centre de
Création Industrielle
AM2003-3

[p. 45]
Yves Saint Laurent
Coat
Spring–Summer 1967
Raffia and macramé collar
with wooden beads
Musée Yves Saint Laurent
– Paris
HC1967E091

[p. 48]
Alberto Giacometti
Man and Woman
1928–29
Bronze, 40 × 40 × 16.5 cm
Paris, Centre Pompidou,
Musée National d'Art
Moderne – Centre de
Création Industrielle,
accepted in lieu, 1984
AM 1984-355

[p. 49]
Yves Saint Laurent
Full-length evening gown
Spring–Summer 1967
Organza with rhodoid
and wooden beads
Musée Yves Saint Laurent
– Paris
HC1967E108

[p. 50]
Robert Delaunay
Rhythm, Joie de vivre
1930
Oil on canvas, 200 × 228 cm
Paris, Centre Pompidou,
Musée National d'Art
Moderne – Centre de
Création Industrielle, gift
of Sonia Delaunay and
Charles Delaunay, 1964
AM 4083 P

[p. 51]
Yves Saint Laurent
'Homage to Pablo
Picasso' gown
Autumn–Winter 1979–80
Moiré faille with satin and
faille appliqué decoration,
satin belt
Musée Yves Saint Laurent
– Paris
HC1979H133

[p. 54]
Piet Mondrian
*Composition in Red, Blue
and White II*, 1937
Oil on canvas, 75 × 60.5 cm
Paris, Centre Pompidou,
Musée National d'Art
Moderne – Centre de
Création Industrielle,
purchase, 1975
AM 1975-53

[p. 55]
Yves Saint Laurent
'Homage to Piet Mondrian'
dress
Autumn–Winter 1965–66
Wool jersey in cream, black,
red, yellow and blue
Musée Yves Saint Laurent
– Paris
HC1965H081

[p. 56]
Henri Matisse
The Romanian Blouse
1940
Oil on canvas, 92 × 73 cm
Paris, Centre Pompidou,
Musée National d'Art
Moderne – Centre de
Création Industrielle, gift of
the artist to the State, 1953
AM 3245 P

[p. 57]
Yves Saint Laurent
Ensemble inspired by
Henri Matisse
Autumn–Winter 1981–82
Wool muslin blouse
embroidered with sequins,
beads and chenille;
velvet skirt; velvet and
passementerie belt
Musée Yves Saint Laurent
Paris
HC1981H072

[p. 58]
Fernand Léger
Polychrome Flower
1952
Cement and painted plaster,
165 × 132 × 47 cm
Paris, Centre Pompidou,
Musée National d'Art
Moderne – Centre de
Création Industrielle,
purchased by the State, 1954
AM 977 S

[p. 59]
Yves Saint Laurent
'Homage to Fernand
Léger' gown
Autumn–Winter 1981–82
Black velvet bodice; faille
skirt with satin and taffeta
appliqué.
Musée Yves Saint Laurent
– Paris
HC1981H148

[p. 60, not exhibited]
Jackson Pollock
The Deep
1953
Oil and enamel on canvas,
220.4 × 150.2 cm
Paris, Centre Pompidou,
Musée National d'Art
Moderne – Centre
de Création Industrielle,
gift made in memory of Jean
de Menil by his children and
the Menil Foundation, 1976
AM 1976-1230

[p. 61, not exhibited]
Yves Saint Laurent
Coat
1984
White ostrich feathers
with black-dyed tips,
on silk organza
Musée Yves Saint Laurent
– Paris
2014.01.36

[p. 62]
Martial Raysse
*Made in Japan –
La Grande Odalisque*
1964
Acrylic paint, glass, plastic
fly and synthetic fibre braid
on photograph mounted on
canvas, 130 × 97 cm
Paris, Centre Pompidou,
Musée National d'Art
Moderne – Centre de
Création Industrielle, gift of
the Scaler Foundation, 1995
AM 1995-213

[p. 63]
Yves Saint Laurent
Coat
Spring–Summer 1971
Green fox fur
Musée Yves Saint Laurent
– Paris
HC1971E090

[p. 64]
Martial Raysse
America America
1964
Neon and painted metal
240 × 165 × 45 cm
Paris, Centre Pompidou,
Musée National d'Art
Moderne – Centre de
Création Industrielle,
purchased 1977
AM 1977-557

[p. 65]
Yves Saint Laurent
'Homage to Pop art' dress
Autumn–Winter 1966–67
Wool jersey in navy,
pink and green
Musée Yves Saint Laurent
– Paris
HC1966H051

[p. 68]
Victor Vasarely
Alom (Dream)
1966
Collage on plywood,
252 × 252 cm
Paris, Centre Pompidou,
Musée National d'Art
Moderne – Centre
de Création Industrielle,
gift of the artist, 1977
AM 1977-229

[p. 69]
Yves Saint Laurent
Dress
Autumn–Winter 1968–69
Wool muslin with geometric
print in brown, orange
and blue.
Musée Yves Saint Laurent
– Paris
HC1968H018

[p. 70]
Yves Saint Laurent
Jumpsuit
Spring–Summer 1970
Silk crepe with geometric
print in black, white
and brown.
Musée Yves Saint Laurent
– Paris
HC1970E054

[p. 71]
Yves Saint Laurent
Dress
Spring–Summer 1969
Black silk crepe with orange
and white dot print.
Musée Yves Saint Laurent
– Paris
HC1969E084

[p. 73]
Ellsworth Kelly
Black White
1988
Oil on canvas, 224 × 231.5 cm
Paris, Centre Pompidou,
Musée National d'Art
Moderne – Centre de
Création Industrielle,
gift of the artist, 1992
AM 1992-362

[p. 73]
Yves Saint Laurent
Evening gown
Autumn–Winter 1965–66
Black silk crepe
Musée Yves Saint Laurent
– Paris
HC1965H054

[p. 76]
Gary Hume
The Moon
2009
Gloss paint on aluminium
panel, 244 × 161 cm
Paris, Centre Pompidou,
Musée National d'Art
Moderne – Centre de
Création Industrielle, gift
of Marie-Aline Prat in 2017
AM 2017-408

[p. 77]
Yves Saint Laurent
'Homage to Tom
Wesselmann' dress
Autumn–Winter 1966–67
Wool jersey in purple,
black and pink
Musée Yves Saint Laurent
– Paris
HC1966H105

[p. 80]
Etel Adnan
Untitled
2010
Oil on canvas, 28,2 × 37,6 cm
Paris, Centre Pompidou,
Musée National d'Art
Moderne – Centre
de Création Industrielle,
purchased 2012
AM 2012-1191 (1) [pp. 82–83]:
AM 2012-1191 (4), (5) and (7)

[p. 81]
Yves Saint Laurent
'Homage to Pop art' dress
Autumn–Winter 1966–67
Wool jersey in blue, navy,
yellow and orange
Musée Yves Saint Laurent
– Paris
HC1966H085

[pp. 84–89]
Selection of Polaroids taken
by couture house staff
1979–2002
Musée Yves Saint Laurent
– Paris

Musée d'Art Moderne de Paris

[p. 90]
Andy Warhol
Portraits of Yves Saint Laurent
1972
Screenprinting ink and
polymer paint on canvas,
204 × 204 cm
Musée Yves Saint Laurent
– Paris

[p. 106]
Henri Matisse
The Unfinished Dance
1931
Three panels, oil and
charcoal on canvas,
344 × 402 cm (left panel),
358.2 × 499 cm (centre panel),
344 × 398 cm (right panel).
Left panel: Paris, Centre
Pompidou, Musée National
d'Art Moderne – Centre de
Création Industrielle,
accepted in lieu, 1983,
AM1993-84. Centre and right
panel: Musée d'Art Moderne
de Paris, purchased from the
Pierre Matisse Estate in 1993,
AMVP 2728

[p. 107]
Yves Saint Laurent
Ensemble inspired
by Henri Matisse
Autumn–Winter 1984–85
Loose 'domino' coat in
graduated shades of pale
blue faille and black velvet;
skirt in pearl satin
Musée Yves Saint Laurent
– Paris
HC1984H147

[p. 110]
Henri Matisse
The Dance
1931–33
Three panels, oil on canvas,
340 × 387 cm (left),
355 × 498 cm (centre),
333 × 391 cm (right)
Musée d'Art Moderne
de Paris, purchased from
the artist for the Paris
International Exhibition, 1937
AMVP 1688

[p. 111]
Yves Saint Laurent
Ensemble inspired by
Henri Matisse
Autumn–Winter 1981–82
Bolero and bodice in black
velvet; patchwork skirt in
white moiré with black stripes
Musée Yves Saint Laurent
– Paris
HC1981H144

[p. 100]
Yves Saint Laurent
Gown inspired by
Henri Matisse
Spring–Summer 1982
Gros-grain bodice; taffeta
skirt with taffeta appliqué;
patent leather belt
Musée Yves Saint Laurent
– Paris
HC1982E099

[p. 112]
Jean Dunand
Sports
1935
Part of a set of 5 wall panels
made for the smoking room
on the SS *Normandie* on
the theme of games and
leisure, bas-relief made
up of 45 gilded panels,
total size: 553 × 540 cm
Musée d'Art Moderne
de Paris, purchased in public
sale, Hôtel des Ventes, Paris,
Palais d'Orsay in 1980
AMS 571

[p. 113]
Yves Saint Laurent
Costume worn by Anny
Duperey in the film *Stavisky*
by Alain Resnais, 1974
May 1974
Coat in cream raw silk
and pleated gown in
cream silk crepe
Musée Yves Saint Laurent
– Paris
2013.05.03.01

[p. 114, not exhibited]
Yves Saint Laurent
Costume worn by Anny
Duperey in the film *Stavisky*
by Alain Resnais, 1974
Cardigan in ivory wool; polo
shirt in ivory and navy wool;
skirt in ivory wool muslin.
Musée Yves Saint Laurent
– Paris
2013.05.06.01

[p. 115]
Yves Saint Laurent
Costume worn by Anny
Duperey in the film *Stavisky*
by Alain Resnais, 1974
May 1974
Jacket and skirt in black wool
crepe; black chiffon blouse
Musée Yves Saint Laurent
– Paris
2013.05.04.01

[p. 116]
Pierre Bonnard
The Garden
c. 1936
Oil on canvas, 127 × 100 cm
Musée d'Art Moderne
de Paris, purchased
from the artist in 1937
AMVP 2539

[p. 117]
Yves Saint Laurent
Ensemble inspired by
Pierre Bonnard
Spring–Summer 2001
Organza blouse with mauve
and magenta print; organza
skirt with pink,
violet and blue print
Musée Yves Saint Laurent
– Paris
HC2001E069

[p. 118]
Yves Saint Laurent
Ensemble inspired
by Pierre Bonnard
Spring–Summer 2001
Organza blouse with red
and orange print; organza
skirt with yellow, pink
and orange print
Musée Yves Saint Laurent
– Paris
HC2001E071

[p. 120]
Raoul Dufy
La Fée Électricité
1937
250 panels
Oil on plywood
Musée d'Art Moderne
de Paris
AMVP 1

[p. 121]
Yves Saint Laurent
Full-length evening ensemble
Autumn–Winter 1992–93
Absinthe satin jacket
and fuchsia satin gown
Musée Yves Saint Laurent
– Paris
HC1992H042 / HC1992H040

[p. 122]
Yves Saint Laurent
Full-length evening ensemble
Autumn–Winter 1992–93
Bronze satin jacket and
emerald satin gown
Musée Yves Saint Laurent
– Paris
HC1992H039 / HC1992H042

[p. 123]
Yves Saint Laurent
Full-length evening ensemble
Autumn–Winter 1992–93
Buttercup satin jacket
and green satin gown
Musée Yves Saint Laurent
– Paris
HC1992H040 / HC1995H075

[p. 124]
Lucio Fontana
*Neon Structure for the
9th Milan Triennale*
1951
White neon tubing,
HT power transformer,
330 × 832 × 832 cm
Reconstruction authorized
by the Fondazione Lucio
Fontana, 2012–14, deposit
no. 2015-AMVPDEP-1

[p. 125]
Yves Saint Laurent
Paletot jacket
Autumn–Winter 1983–84
Black velvet embroidered
with silver 'dust'
Musée Yves Saint Laurent
– Paris
HC1983H140

[p. 126]
Yves Saint Laurent
Blouse
Autumn–Winter 1962–63
Pearl grey satin
Musée Yves Saint Laurent
– Paris
HC1962H106

[p. 127]
Yves Saint Laurent
Gown
Silver grey panne velvet
Autumn–Winter 1975–76
Musée Yves Saint Laurent
– Paris
HC1975H072

[p. 128]
Alain Jacquet
Le Déjeuner sur l'herbe
1964
Diptych, four-colour
screenprint on canvas
Musée d'Art Moderne
de Paris, purchased in 1989
AMVP 2685

[p. 129]
Yves Saint Laurent
Jacket
Spring–Summer 1966
Jacquard wool in white,
blue and black
Musée Yves Saint Laurent
– Paris
HC1966E046

[p. 131]
Yves Saint Laurent
Pea coat
Spring–Summer 1966
Jacquard wool in
navy and white
Musée Yves Saint Laurent
– Paris
HC1966E019

[p. 131]
Yves Saint Laurent
Dress
Spring–Summer 1969
Black, green and
white silk crepe
Musée Yves Saint Laurent
– Paris
HC1969E082

[p. 131]
Yves Saint Laurent
Jacket
Spring–Summer 1966
Jacquard wool in green and
white
Musée Yves Saint Laurent
– Paris
HC1966E047

[p. 134 left]
Giorgio de Chirico
Idillio antico (Ancient Idyll)
c. 1970
Oil on canvas, 55 × 46 cm
Musée d'Art Moderne
de Paris, legacy of Isabella
Pakszwer De Chirico in 2011
AMVP 3552

[p. 134 right]
Giorgio de Chirico
Piazza d'Italia with Statue
n. d.
Oil on canvas,
40 × 41.5 cm
Musée d'Art Moderne
de Paris, legacy of Isabella
Pakszwer De Chirico in 2011
AMVP 3534

[p. 135]
Yves Saint Laurent
Coat
Autumn–Winter 1968–69
Black chenille wool with
astrakhan effect
Musée Yves Saint Laurent
– Paris
HC1968H033

[p. 137]
Yves Saint Laurent
Dress
Spring–Summer 1971
Silk crepe with marbled
green print motif
Musée Yves Saint Laurent
– Paris
HC1971E066

[pp. 138–139]
Yves Saint Laurent
Set designs for the library
in *The Two-Headed Eagle*
by Jean Cocteau
1978
Musée Yves Saint Laurent
– Paris
2012.01.1413,
2012.01.1203
and 2012.01.1201

[p. 142]
Daniel Buren
Wall of Paintings
1995
Set of 20 canvases painted
between 1966 and 1977
Acrylic paint on cotton
canvas with alternating
stripes, each 8.7 cm wide,
canvas dimensions vary
Musée d'Art Moderne
de Paris, purchased in 2000
with the support of Marc
Martin-Malburet and
the SAMAMVP
AMVP 2832

[p. 143]
Yves Saint Laurent
Coat dress
Spring–Summer 1970
Denim
Saint Laurent Rive
Gauche collection
Musée Yves Saint Laurent
– Paris
RG1970E931

List of works exhibited

Musée du Louvre

[p. 144]
Jacques Henri Lartigue
Yves Saint Laurent
2 February 1976
Silver print on coated paper
Musée Yves Saint Laurent
– Paris
PH1976LAR01.01

[p. 157]
Yves Saint Laurent
'Heart' necklace'
Smoky grey rhinestones,
red crystal cabochons,
white pearls and red glass
pendant, designed in 1962
and recreated in 1979
by Maison Scemama
Musée Yves Saint Laurent
– Paris

[p. 160]
Yves Saint Laurent
'Broken Mirror' jacket
Black velvet embroidered
with gold, silver and rhodoid
Autumn–Winter 1978–79
Musée Yves Saint Laurent
– Paris
HC1978H097

[p. 161]
Yves Saint Laurent
Jacket
Black gazar with gold
embroidery
Spring–Summer 1980
Musée Yves Saint Laurent
– Paris
HC1980E067

[p. 164]
Yves Saint Laurent
Jacket
Organza embroidered
with sequins, rhinestones
and chenille
Autumn–Winter 1981–82
Musée Yves Saint Laurent
– Paris
HC1981H138

[p. 165]
Yves Saint Laurent
'Homage to My House' jacket
Organza embroidered with
gold and rock crystal
Spring–Summer 1990
Musée Yves Saint Laurent
– Paris
HC1990E113

Musée d'Orsay

[p. 170]
Lord Snowdon
Yves Saint Laurent
Deauville, 1980
Chromogenic print
With the kind permission
of Frances von Hofmannsthal

[p. 183 left]
Yves Saint Laurent
Tuxedo
Autumn–Winter 1966–67
Black grain de poudre and silk
satin; blouse in white organdy
Musée Yves Saint Laurent
– Paris
HC1966H076

[p. 183 right]
Yves Saint Laurent
Tuxedo
Spring–Summer 1967
Black wool gabardine;
waistcoat and shirt in
white cotton piqué
Musée Yves Saint Laurent
– Paris
HC1967E088

[p. 184]
Yves Saint Laurent
Tuxedo
Spring–Summer 1967
Navy alpaca; blouse in white
organdy with plum satin bow.
Musée Yves Saint Laurent
– Paris
HC1967E056

[not illustrated]
Yves Saint Laurent
Tuxedo
Autumn–Winter 1998–99
Black grain de poudre;
white satin blouse
Musée Yves Saint Laurent
– Paris
HC1998H032

[p. 185]
Yves Saint Laurent
Tuxedo
Autumn–Winter 2001–2
Black velvet; blouse
in white cotton
Musée Yves Saint Laurent
– Paris
HC2001H037

[p. 187]
Yves Saint Laurent
Gown designed for
Marie-Hélène de Rothschild
on the occasion
of the Bal Proust
1971
Ivory satin with ivory
satin belt and bow
Musée Yves Saint Laurent
– Paris, gift of Marie-Hélène
de Rothschild
2013.06.03

[p. 189]
Yves Saint Laurent
Gown designed for Jane
Birkin on the occasion
of the Bal Proust
1971
Ivory crepe georgette
and white lace with ivory
satin belt and bow.
Musée Yves Saint Laurent
– Paris, gift of Jane Birkin
2013.06.01

[p. 190]
Joseph Paxton
*View of the south and east
facades of the Château
de Ferrières*
1853–56
Pencil, ink and watercolour
on paper with retouching
in white, 41 × 73.5 cm
Paris, Musée d'Orsay,
purchased 2010
ARO 2010 21

[p. 191]
Yves Saint Laurent
Gown design for Marie-
Hélène de Rothschild
1971
Pencil on paper
Musée Yves Saint Laurent
– Paris
2012.01.1710

[pp. 192–193]
Yves Saint Laurent
Sketches for gowns
for the Bal Proust
1971
Pencil on paper
Musée Yves Saint Laurent
– Paris
2019.06.01; 02; 07

[not illustrated]
Yves Saint Laurent
Gown design for Jane
Birkin for the Bal Proust
1971
Graphite and felt-tip on paper
Musée Yves Saint Laurent
– Paris
2012.01.1712 et 1713

[p. 194]
Félix Nadar
Sarah Bernhardt
1859
Salt print from a collodion
glass negative, 21.6 × 17.2 cm
Paris, Musée d'Orsay, gift of
the Kodak-Pathé Foundation,
1983
PHO 1983 165 131

[not illustrated]
Paul Nadar
Portrait of Sarah Bernhardt
c. 1900
Albumen print mounted on
cardboard, 13.5 × 9.5 cm
Paris, Musée d'Orsay, gift
of Jacques-Paul Dauriac
via the Société des Amis
du Musée d'Orsay
(SAMO), 2001
PHO 2001 11 19

[not illustrated]
Paul Nadar
Polaire
c. 1890
Albumen print
mounted on cardboard
Paris, Musée d'Orsay,
gift of Madame Daphné
Doublet-Vaudoyer, 1988
PHO 1988 28 7

[not illustrated]
Paul Nadar
Portrait of Dortzal
c. 1900
Albumen print
mounted on cardboard
Paris, Musée d'Orsay, gift
of Jacques-Paul Dauriac
via la Société des Amis
du Musée d'Orsay
(SAMO), 2001
PHO 2001 11 11

[not illustrated]
Paul Nadar
Liane de Pougy
1904
Albumen print
mounted on cardboard
Paris, Musée d'Orsay,
gift of Madame Daphné
Doublet-Vaudoyer, 1988
PHO 1988 28 8

[p. 195]
Cecil Beaton
Baroness de Rothschild
1971
Cecil Beaton Archives

[p. 196]
Cecil Beaton
Hélène Rochas
1971
Cecil Beaton Archives

[p. 197]
Cecil Beaton
Marisa Berenson
1971
Cecil Beaton Archives

[p. 198]
Cecil Beaton
Jacqueline de Ribes
1971
Cecil Beaton Archives

[p. 199]
Cecil Beaton
Jane Birkin
1971
Cecil Beaton Archives

[p. 200, not exhibited]
Claude Monet
Le Déjeuner sur l'herbe
1865–66
Oil on canvas, 418 × 378 cm
Paris, Musée d'Orsay,
gift, 1957 and accepted
in lieu, 1987
RF 1957 7 and RF 1987 12

[p. 201, not exhibited]
Yves Saint Laurent
'Je vivrai un grand amour'
bridal gown
Spring–Summer 1986
White faille with black
dot print
Musée Yves Saint Laurent
– Paris
HC1986E098

[p. 203, not exhibited]
Yves Saint Laurent
Trouser suit
Spring–Summer 1978
Grey herringbone wool;
blouse in white crepe
de Chine
Musée Yves Saint Laurent
– Paris
HC1978E002

[pp. 206–211]
Yves Saint Laurent
Sketches for costumes for
the Queen and Édith de Berg
in *The Two-Headed Eagle*
by Jean Cocteau
1978
Felt-tip and pastel on paper
Musée Yves Saint Laurent
– Paris
2012.01.0970; 0971; 0975;
0976; 1979;1005
2012.01.0969; 1032; 1039;
1040; 1041

[pp. 212–215]
Yves Saint Laurent
Sketches for headdresses
and decorations for the
Bal des Têtes
1957
Gouache, pastels, ink
and pencil on paper
Musée Yves Saint Laurent
– Paris
2012.01.0756; 0758-0763;
0765; 0766; 0768

Musée National Picasso, Paris

[p. 216]
Irving Penn
Yves Saint Laurent
2 August 1983
Musée Yves Saint Laurent
– Paris
PH1983PEN01.01

[p. 230]
Pablo Picasso
Violin
Paris, 1915
Cut and folded sheet
metal, paint and wire,
100 × 63.7 × 18 cm
Musée National Picasso-
Paris, accepted in lieu
from Pablo Picasso, 1979
MP255

[p. 231 left]
Yves Saint Laurent
'Homage to Pablo Picasso'
jacket
Spring–Summer 1988
Ottoman wool, embroidered
with beads and sequins
Musée Yves Saint Laurent
– Paris
HC1988E065

[p. 231 right]
Yves Saint Laurent
'Homage to Pablo Picasso'
jacket
Spring–Summer 1988
Black ottoman wool,
embroidered with
beads and sequins
Musée Yves Saint Laurent
– Paris
HC1988E059

[p. 234]
Pablo Picasso
Portrait of Nusch Éluard
Paris, Autumn 1937
Oil on canvas, 92 × 65.2 cm
Musée National Picasso-
Paris, accepted in lieu from
Jacqueline Picasso, 1990
MP1990-19

[p. 235]
Yves Saint Laurent
'Homage to Pablo Picasso'
jacket
Autumn–Winter 1979–80
Black, black and ivory wool
Musée Yves Saint Laurent
– Paris
HC1979H005

[p. 238]
Pablo Picasso
*Bust of a Woman
in a Striped Hat*
Paris, 3 June 1939
Tempera on hardboard,
81 × 54 cm
Musée National Picasso-
Paris, accepted in lieu
from Pablo Picasso, 1979
MP180

[p. 239]
Yves Saint Laurent
'Homage to Pablo
Picasso' dress
Autumn–Winter 1979–80
Black satin and velvet,
embroidered with
sequins and beads
Musée Yves Saint Laurent
– Paris
HC1979H077

Musée Yves Saint Laurent Paris

[p. 4]
Cassandre (Adolphe
Jean-Marie Mouron)
Logo for the Yves Saint
Laurent couture house
1961
Gouache on paper
Musée Yves Saint Laurent
– Paris
PB.YSL.AG.008

[p. 240]
Andy Warhol
Yves Saint Laurent
1979
Graphite on paper
Musée Yves Saint Laurent
– Paris
PB.YSL.AG.006

[pp. 250–253]
Yves Saint Laurent
Sketches chosen by the
couturier for his farewell
show at the Centre Pompidou
on 20 January 2002, 1962–2002,
graphite, felt-tip and/or
pastel on paper.
Musée Yves Saint Laurent
– Paris

[p. 254]
Toile for a jacket made
between 1980 and 2002
Cotton with pencil
annotations and
fabric swatch
Musée Yves Saint Laurent
– Paris

[p. 255 left]
Atelier Madame Colette
Toile for a gown with
allover embroidery
Spring–Summer 2001
White cotton gauze
and black fabric appliqué
Musée Yves Saint Laurent
– Paris
HC2001E086

[p. 255 right]
Atelier Monsieur Jean-Pierre
Toile for a tuxedo-style
jumpsuit
Autumn–Winter 2000-1
Cotton and black ribbon
Musée Yves Saint Laurent
– Paris
HC2000H040

[p. 257]
Atelier Madame Jacqueline
Toile for a 'Homage to
Georges Braque' cape
Spring–Summer 1988
Cotton and photocopy
Musée Yves Saint Laurent
– Paris
HC1988E127

[p. 258]
Atelier Madame Colette
Toile for an ensemble
inspired by Henri Matisse
Autumn–Winter 1999–2000
Cotton and photocopy
Musée Yves Saint Laurent
– Paris
HC1999H056

[p. 259]
Atelier Madame Catherine
Toile for a 'Homage to
Georges Braque' gown
Spring–Summer 1988
Cotton, cardboard
and pastels
Musée Yves Saint Laurent
– Paris
HC1988E117

[p. 260]
Atelier Monsieur Jean-Pierre
Toile for a 'Homage to
Georges Braque' cape
Spring–Summer 1988
Cotton and pastels
Musée Yves Saint Laurent
– Paris
HC1988E119

[p. 261]
Atelier Monsieur Jean-Pierre
Toile for a 'Homage to
Georges Braque' cape
Spring–Summer 1988
Cotton and pastels
Musée Yves Saint Laurent
– Paris
HC1988E123

[p. 262]
Atelier Monsieur Alain
Toile for a 'Homage to
Georges Braque' cape
Spring–Summer 1988
Cotton, graphite and
black fabric appliqué
Musée Yves Saint Laurent
– Paris
HC1988E128

[p. 263]
Atelier Monsieur Jean-Pierre
Toile for a 'Homage to
Pablo Picasso' jacket
Spring–Summer 1988
Cotton, black pencil
and pastels
Musée Yves Saint Laurent
– Paris
HC1988E058

[p. 265]
Atelier Monsieur Yuksel
Toile for a 'Homage to
Pablo Picasso' jacket
Spring–Summer 1988
Cotton, graphite and
fabric appliqué
Musée Yves Saint Laurent
– Paris
HC1988E065

[pp. 266–267]
Envelopes filled with sewing
patterns, marked with the
name of the *premier d'atelier*,
the season, the collection
and the design number
Musée Yves Saint Laurent
– Paris

[p. 268]
Atelier Monsieur Jean-Marie
Pattern for a blouse,
3 of 4 pieces
Autumn–Winter 1990–91
Cotton and felt-tip
Musée Yves Saint Laurent
– Paris
HC1990H038

[p. 269 above]
Atelier Monsieur Jean-Marie
Pattern for a jacket,
3 of 9 pieces
Autumn–Winter 1990
Cotton and felt-tip
Musée Yves Saint Laurent
– Paris
HC1990H065

[p. 269 below left]
Atelier Monsieur Jean-Marie
Pattern for a jacket,
4 of 11 pieces
Autumn–Winter 1990–91
Cotton and felt-tip
Musée Yves Saint Laurent
– Paris
HC1990H043

[p. 269 below right]
Atelier Monsieur Jean-Marie
Pattern for a pea coat,
1 of 7 pieces
Spring–Summer 1990
Cotton and felt-tip
HC1990H002

[p. 270]
Polaroid taken by
couture house staff,
Autumn–Winter 1985–86

[p. 271]
Shoe forms
Wood and graphite
Musée Yves Saint Laurent
– Paris

[pp. 272–273]
Shoe patterns
1962–80
Paper, felt-tip and graphite
Musée Yves Saint Laurent
– Paris

[pp. 276–277]
Hat forms and hat blocks
Plant fibre, graphite and wood
1962–2002
Musée Yves Saint Laurent
– Paris

[pp. 278–279]
Embroidery and appliqué
swatches commissioned
by Yves Saint Laurent,
made by Lanel, Lesage,
Montex and other French
embroidery workshops
1962–2002
Musée Yves Saint Laurent
– Paris

[pp. 280–281]
Original prints for Yves
Saint Laurent scarves, made
by the Maison Abraham
1970s, screenprint
on blotting paper
Musée Yves Saint Laurent
– Paris

[p. 282]
Naomi Campbell wearing
the 'Homage to Vincent
Van Gogh' jacket
Polaroid taken by
couture house staff
Spring–Summer 1988
Musée Yves Saint Laurent
– Paris

[p. 283]
Yves Saint Laurent,
'Homage to Vincent
Van Gogh' jacket
Spring–Summer 1988
Embroidered with sequins,
beads and ribbon by the
Maison Lesage
Musée Yves Saint Laurent
– Paris
HC1988E094

Selected bibliography

This bibliography features a broad selection of exhibition catalogues published since 1983,
the date of the first exhibition of Yves Saint Laurent's work, held at the
Metropolitan Museum of Art, New York.

Exhibition catalogues

Yves Saint Laurent,
(ed. Diana Vreeland),
Metropolitan Museum of Art,
New York; New York:
Clarkson N. Potter, 1983

Yves Saint Laurent 1958–1985,
National Art Museum of
China, Beijing; Paris:
Yves Saint Laurent S.A, 1985

*Yves Saint Laurent par
Yves Saint Laurent,*
Musée des Arts de la Mode,
Paris; Paris: Musée des
Arts de la Mode/Herscher,
1986

Yves Saint Laurent et le théâtre,
Musée des Arts Décoratifs,
Paris; Paris: Musée des Arts
Décoratifs/Herscher, 1986

*Yves Saint Laurent
Retrospective,* Art Gallery of
New South Wales, Sydney;
Sydney: Art Gallery of
New South Wales, 1987

*Yves Saint Laurent:
Mode 1958–1990,* Sezon
Museum of Modern Art,
Karuizawa; Karuizawa: Sezon
Museum of Modern Art, 1990

Yves Saint Laurent. Exotismes,
Musée de la Mode – Espace
Mode Méditerranée,
Marseilles; Marseilles:
Musée de la Mode; Paris:
Réunion des Musées
Nationaux, 1993

*40 ans de création en dentelle.
Yves Saint Laurent,
haute couture,* Musées
des Beaux-Arts de la
Dentelle, Alençon; Alençon:
Musée des Beaux-Arts
de la Dentelle, 2002

*Yves Saint Laurent,
Dialogue avec l'art,*
Fondation Pierre Bergé
–Yves Saint Laurent,
Paris; Paris: Fondation
Pierre Bergé –Yves
Saint Laurent, 2004

*Yves Saint Laurent.
Smoking forever,*
Fondation Pierre Bergé –
Yves Saint Laurent, Paris;
Paris: Fondation Pierre
Bergé –Yves Saint
Laurent, 2005

*Yves Saint Laurent.
Voyages extraordinaires,*
Fondation Pierre Bergé –
Yves Saint Laurent, Paris;
Paris: Fondation Pierre
Bergé –Yves Saint
Laurent, 2006

*Nan Kempner. Une
Américaine à Paris,* Fondation
Pierre Bergé –Yves Saint
Laurent, Paris; Paris:
Fondation Pierre Bergé –
Yves Saint Laurent, 2007

*Yves Saint Laurent.
Théâtre, cinéma, music-hall,
ballet,* Fondation Pierre
Bergé –Yves Saint Laurent,
Paris; Paris: Fondation
Pierre Bergé –Yves
Saint Laurent, 2007

Yves Saint Laurent: Style,
Musée des Beaux-Arts,
Montreal; de Young Museum,
San Francisco; Paris:
La Martinière, 2008

*Une Passion marocaine.
Caftans, broderies, bijoux,*
Fondation Pierre Bergé –
Yves Saint Laurent, Paris;
Paris: Connaissance des
Arts, 2009

*Yves Saint Laurent,
Diálogo con el arte,*
Fundación Caixa Galicia,
La Coruña; La Coruña:
Fundación Caixa Galicia;
Paris: Fondation Pierre Bergé
–Yves Saint Laurent, 2008

Yves Saint Laurent,
Petit Palais, Musée
des Beaux-Arts de la Ville
de Paris; Paris: La Martinière/
Fondation Pierre Bergé –
Yves Saint Laurent, 2010

*Saint Laurent rive gauche.
La révolution de la mode,*
Fondation Pierre Bergé –
Yves Saint Laurent, Paris;
Paris: La Martinière/
Fondation Pierre Bergé
–Yves Saint Laurent, 2011

Yves Saint Laurent visionnaire,
Centre Culturel ING,
Brussels; Brussels: ING;
Paris, Fondation Pierre Bergé
–Yves Saint Laurent, 2013

*Yves Saint Laurent + Halston.
Fashioning the 70s,* Fashion
Institute of Technology,
New York; New Haven, CT:
Yale University Press, 2015

*Yves Saint Laurent 1971.
La Collection du scandale,*
Fondation Pierre Bergé –
Yves Saint Laurent, Paris;
Paris: Flammarion/Fondation
Pierre Bergé –Yves Saint
Laurent, 2011

*Yves Saint Laurent:
Style is Eternal,* Bowes
Museum, Barnard Castle;
Barnard Castle: Bowes
Museum; Paris: Fondation
Pierre Bergé –Yves Saint
Laurent, 2015

*Yves Saint Laurent: The
Perfection of Style,* Seattle
Art Museum, Seattle;
Virginia Museum of Fine
Arts, Richmond, VA;
New York: Rizzoli, 2017

*L'Asie Rêvée d'Yves
Saint Laurent,* Musée
Yves Saint Laurent Paris;
Musée des Arts Asiatiques,
Nice; Paris: Gallimard, 2018;
English ed.: *Yves Saint
Laurent: Dreams of the
Orient,* London: Thames
& Hudson, 2018

*Yves Saint Laurent,
Les coulisses de la haute
couture à Lyon,* Musée
Yves Saint Laurent Paris;
Lyons: Libel, 2019

*Betty Catroux, Yves Saint
Laurent – féminin singulier,*
Musée Yves Saint Laurent
Paris; Paris: Gallimard/
Musée Yves Saint Laurent
Paris, 2020

This book was published on the occasion of the exhibition 'Yves Saint Laurent aux musées', presented at the Centre Pompidou, the Musée d'Art Moderne de Paris, the Musée du Louvre, the Musée d'Orsay, the Musée National Picasso, Paris and the Musée Yves Saint Laurent – Paris.

29 January 2022–15 May 2022*

*At the Musée du Louvre and Centre Pompidou, until 16 May 2022.
At the Musée National Picasso, Paris, the exhibition will close on 10 April 2022.
At the Musée Yves Saint Laurent – Paris, the exhibition will be extended until 18 September 2022.

The entire project was supported by the Fondation Pierre Bergé – Yves Saint Laurent. The designs exhibited at the participating museums are part of the unique legacy left by Yves Saint Laurent and Pierre Bergé when the couture house closed in 2002, which is now conserved and safeguarded by the Fondation for the benefit of everyone.

Exhibition

Curators

Madison Cox,
  president of the
  Fondation Pierre Bergé
  – Yves Saint Laurent
Stephan Janson (S.J.),
  fashion designer
Mouna Mekouar (M.M.),
  art historian and
  freelance curator

Advisory committee

Laurent Le Bon,
  president of the
  Centre Pompidou
Fabrice Hergott,
  director of the Musée
  d'Art Moderne de Paris
Laurence Descars,
  president of the
  Musée du Louvre
Cécile Debray,
  president of the Musée
  National Picasso, Paris
Christophe Leribault,
  president of the
  Musée d'Orsay

**Associate curators
by institution**

Centre Pompidou
Christian Briend,
  chief curator, head of
  modern collections
Marie Sarré (M.S.),
  associate curator,
  modern collections

MAM – Paris Musées
Charlotte Barat (C.B.),
  exhibition curator,
  historical collections

Musée du Louvre
Anne Dion-Tenenbaum,
  chief curator, Objets
  d'Art department
Exhibition commissioned
and overseen by:
Dominique de Font-Réaulx,
  director of mediation and
  cultural programming

Musée d'Orsay
Anaïs Alchus (A.A.),
  curator of decorative arts

**Musée National Picasso,
Paris**
Émilia Philippot,
  head of collections
  and mediation

**Musée Yves Saint Laurent
– Paris**
Aurélie Samuel (A.S.),
  chief curator and director
  of collections

Assisted by:
Alice Coulon-Saillard
  (A.C.-S.), manager of
  photography collections
Domille Éblé (D.É.),
  manager of graphic
  art collections
Judith Lamas,
  manager of textile
  collections

Exhibition design:
Jasmin Oezcebi

General manager:
Luz Gyalui

Installation:
LUMIDÉCO

Lighting design:
ACL, Transpalux

Textiles conservation:
Nataly Herrera
  assisted by
Montse de Mateo Puigmartí
Léa Denys
Célia Thibaud

Graphic art and
photography conservation:
Élodie Remazeilles
Marie Beutter-Panhard

Communications:
Claudine Colin
Alexis Grégorat

Graphic design:
H5
Lacasta Design

Signage:
Oeil de Lynx

Photographs:
Nicolas Mathéus

Musée Yves Saint Laurent Paris

Elsa Janssen
  museum director
Laurent Gardette,
  administrative and financial
  director

Conservation
Aurélie Samuel,
  chief curator and director
  of collections
Alice Coulon-Saillard,
  manager of photography
  and audiovisual collections
Domitille Eblé, manager of
  graphic art collections
Judith Lamas, manager of
  textiles and accessories
  collections

**Exhibition and
collection logistics**
Joséphine Imbault,
  logistics manager
Tiphanie Musset, assistant

**Communications and
visitor management**
Mélanie Scavetta,
  visitor manager

Administration
Alain Darbois, general
  support services
Maria Ribeiro,
  administrative support
Bénédicte Segré, head
  accountant

**Board members of the
Fondation Pierre Bergé –
Yves Saint Laurent**

Madison Cox,
  president
Maxime Catroux,
  vice-president
Peter Blunschi,
  general secretary
Laurent Levasseur,
  treasurer
Francesca Belletini
Philippe de Cossé-Brissac
Antoine Godeau
Laurent Le Bon
Paloma Picasso
Bérangère Primat
Alexander Vreeland
Mustapha Zine

**Board members of the
Musée Yves Saint Laurent
– Paris**

Madison Cox,
  president
Emmanuel Pierrat,
  secretary
Laurent Levasseur,
  treasurer
Patricia Barbizet
Peter Blunschi
Maxime Catroux
Samia Saouma
Laure Morsy
Patrick Martin
Alexander Vreeland

Acknowledgments

The Fondation Pierre Bergé – Yves Saint Laurent would like to thank:

Aube Breton Elléouët
Marie-Andrée Corcuff

Maison Lemarié
Maison Lesage

Françoise Picoli
Christelle Posada

Centre Pompidou
Julie Narbey,
  general director
Xavier Rey, director of MNAM
Brigitte Léal,
  deputy director,
  head of collections
Claire Garnier,
  head of production
Agnès Benayer,
  head of communication
  and digital
Lydia Poitevin,
  head of public relations
Marine Prévot,
  press officer
Tara Benveniste,
  social media manager
Roxane Venditti,
  public relations manager
Céline Makragic,
  collection support
Yannick Château,
  collection support
Pierre-Emmanuel Potey,
  collection support
Dominique Fasquel,
  lighting designer

We would also like to
thank Serge Lasvignes and
Bernard Blistère for their
enthusiasm and support
since the launch of this
project in December 2020.

MAM – Paris Musées
Anne-Sophie de Gasquet,
  general director
  of Paris Musées
Julie Bertrand,
  director of exhibitions and
  publications, Paris Musées

Laurie Szulc,
  general secretary
Laurent Santucci,
  deputy general secretary
Annabelle Constant,
  head of culture department
Claire Schillinger,
  head of communication
Maud Ohana,
  press manager
Peggy Delahalle,
  communications officer
Madalen Hulin,
  communications assistant
Claire Böhm,
  head of exhibition and
  collection logistics
  department
Carmen Sokolenko,
  exhibition coordinator

Musée d'Orsay
Sylvie Patry,
  chief curator, head
  of conservation
  and collections
Pierre-Emmanuel Lecerf,
  general manager
Virginie Donzeaud,
  deputy general manager
Jean Naudin,
  interim head of exhibitions
Stéphanie de Brabander,
  exhibitions manager
Odile Michel,
  head of collection
  logistics department
Agathe Boucleinville,
  head of architecture,
  maintenance and
  building security
Milan Dargent,
  head of hospitality
  and monitoring
Guillaume Blanc,
  head of visitor management
Luc Bouniol-Laffont,
  head of cultural
  programming and
  event spaces
Hélène Charbonnier,
  head of digital
Guillaume Roux,
  head of development
Amélie Hardivillier,
  head of communications,
  assisted by Gabrielle
  Lacombe and Cécile
  Castagnola

Musée du Louvre
Dominique de Font-Réaulx,
  director of mediation and
  cultural programming
Aline François-Colin,
  deputy director
Jannic Durand,
  head of Objets d'Art
  department
Anne Dion-Tenenbaum,
  lead curator, Objets d'Art
  department
Marie-Julie Chastang,
  head of exhibitions
  department
Claire Chalvet,
  project coordinator
Karima Hammache-Rezzouk,
  head of project
  management department
David Burban,
  works manager
Aline Cymbler,
  head of the museum
  workshops department
Sébastien Née,
  head of lighting workshop
Éric Journée,
  head of painting workshop
Pascal Goujet,
  head of exhibit display
  workshop
Sophie Grange,
  assistant head of
  communications
Jeanne Scanvic,
  communications officer
Carole Manzano,
  deputy head of architecture,
  museum management
  and signage
Frédérique Althey,
  graphic designer

**Musée National Picasso,
Paris**
Marie Bauer,
  head of communications
  department
Léa Delaroche,
  communications officer
Alexandre Therwath,
  head of culture department
Alix Maraval,
  programming officer
Sophie Daynes-Diallo,
  head of production
  department
Sarah Lagrevol,
  collection logistics
Delphine Cazus,
  collection logistics

Translated from the French *Yves Saint Laurent aux musées* by Ruth Sharman

First published in the United Kingdom in 2022 by
Thames & Hudson Ltd, 181A High Holborn, London WC1V 7QX

First published in the United States of America in 2022 by
Thames & Hudson Inc., 500 Fifth Avenue, New York, New York 10110

Original edition © 2022 Editions Gallimard, Paris
This edition © 2022 Thames & Hudson Ltd, London

British Library Cataloguing-in-Publication Data.
A catalogue record for this book is available from the British Library

Library of Congress Control Number 2021949691

ISBN 978-0-500-02544-4

Printed in Belgium

Be the first to know about our new releases,
exclusive content and author events by visiting
thamesandhudson.com
thamesandhudsonusa.com
thamesandhudson.com.au